To Tom & Lisa
with very best wishes
Noel

© Noel Hudson and St Ives Town Council, 1989

All rights reserved. No part of this publication may be reproduced, stored in a retrieval system, or transmitted in any form or by any means, electrical, mechanical, photocopying, recording or otherwise, without the permission of the copyright owners. Enquiries should be addressed to the publisher.

First published 1989

ISBN 0 9515298 0 3

St Ives Town Council
Town Hall
Market Hill
St Ives, Huntingdon
Cambridgeshire PE17 4AN

Printed and bound in Great Britain by Black Bear Press, Cambridge

Acknowledgements

I am indebted to a great many people for the help and cooperation they gave me while I was researching and writing this book. Given a limited amount of time in which to produce the manuscript, I needed this assistance and everyone I approached for help responded generously.

I owe a particular debt of gratitude to Sue Edgington, a world authority on the life of St Ivo. Not only did she give me invaluable help and guidance, but she allowed me full use of her translation of Goscelin's Life and Miracles of St Ivo.

My friend Dickie Butterfield of Hemingford Abbots wrote virtually the entire chapter on prehistoric St Ives for me. Bob Burn-Murdoch, the curator of the Norris Museum, also contributed to the chapter.

Every councillor I approached extended cooperation. Among them were mayor Mark Plews, deputy mayor Jean Chandler, Pru Pegram, Rex Wadsworth, Taffy James and Peter Anderson. Mary Grove, Ethel Cuttill and Michael Barton, veterans of the former borough council, also came to my aid. Michael Barton very kindly lent me interesting old ledgers relating to the chemist shop members of his family ran for more than a century.

The church rallied round. The Rev. David Moore and Canon Jennings kept me straight about All Saints. The Rev John Ballard and the Rev Donald McIlhagga gave invaluable advice about the Free Church, as did Mary Carter whose own book on the church appeared a few years ago. The Rev Mark Goodhand and Father Raymond Kerby guided me on Methodism and Roman Catholicism respectively, and I must not forget the Rev Ian Suttie who allowed me to use material from his unpublished thesis on Methodism in St Ives.

The list is almost endless. Town Clerk Anthony Watson gave me a welcome guiding hand, and E. P. (Ted) Brand of Ramsey encouraged me to research the material for the chapter on Ramsey Abbey.

Other people who were generous with their time included David Bryant and Joe Johnson, while Robert Flack, of Westfield School kindly allowed me to use his unpublished material on the international fair. From Quebec I received unstinted help and encouragement from Ellen Wedemeyer Moore, an authority on the medieval fairs of England. Buoyant Robin Kiddle was of great assistance when it came to writing about the old clock tower with whose history his family was closely associated.

My thanks are also due to Philip Saunders and Kate Chantry of the Huntingdon Records Office and also to the staff of the Cambridgeshire Records Office in Shire Hall.

I spent many hours with Freddy Favell, the former assistant town clerk to the borough council, whose remarkable memory of events in St Ives extends back more than 70 years.

Finally I must confess this book would never have been researched and written in the allotted time were it not for Bob Burn-Murdoch. Not only did he contribute material to the second chapter, but throughout the year he bore with limitless patience endless interruptions to his daily work. He also encouraged, guided and helped me in innumerable ways. His help was invaluable.

By the same author:
Catherine the Great to Wordsworth. 100 Years of Huntingdon Steeplechasing.

The illustrations were provided by the following: Norris Museum, figs. 2, 3, 4a, 5, 6b, 7, 11, 12b, 13, 14, 15a, 16, 17a, 18b, 19a–c; Brian Jones, figs. 1, 4b, 8a, 10, 12a, 15c, 17b–c, 18a; Stuart Hodgson, figs. 6a, 9; Martin Cannon, fig. 8b; Canon Jennings, fig. 15b; Freddy Favell, fig. 19d; Tim George, fig. 20. Stuart Hodgson also took the photographs for the dust jacket.

Front cover: All Saints Parish Church.
Back cover: The Chapel on the Bridge.

Contents

ACKNOWLEDGEMENTS iii
FOREWORD ix
CHAPTER 1 A Persian Archbishop 1
CHAPTER 2 Prehistoric St Ives 11
CHAPTER 3 The Black Monks 19
CHAPTER 4 Domesday 29
CHAPTER 5 Princelings and Foreign Merchants 33
CHAPTER 6 The Farmer of St Ives 43
CHAPTER 7 A Mischievous Puritan 55
CHAPTER 8 Three Chroniclers 59
CHAPTER 9 John Skeeles 67
CHAPTER 10 Political Passions 79
CHAPTER 11 An Illustrious Market 83
CHAPTER 12 All Saints 93
CHAPTER 13 Nonconformity in St Ives 105
CHAPTER 14 Other Churches 113
CHAPTER 15 A Century of Borough Status 119
CHAPTER 16 1110 and All That 131

Foreword

One hundred years ago Herbert Norris published his collection of notes in "A History of St Ives".

It is fitting that in the centenary year of that publication, St Ives Town Council asked Noel Hudson to write a new and up-to-date history of our Town.

A number of works dealing with St Ives' history have been written since 1889 – notably those by Little and Werba, Dr. Mary Carter, and Bob Burn-Murdoch (who is Curator of the Library and Museum set up by Herbert Norris and now run by St Ives Town Council) – but Noel Hudson's book is a fresh and thoroughly researched account covering from pre-history to this very year.

This new book shows how St Ives has developed from the tiny hamlet of Slepe into the splendid town it is today.

I hope you will enjoy reading it and learn from it – as I have.

MARK PLEWS
TOWN MAYOR

September 1989

To my sons Adam and Matthew.

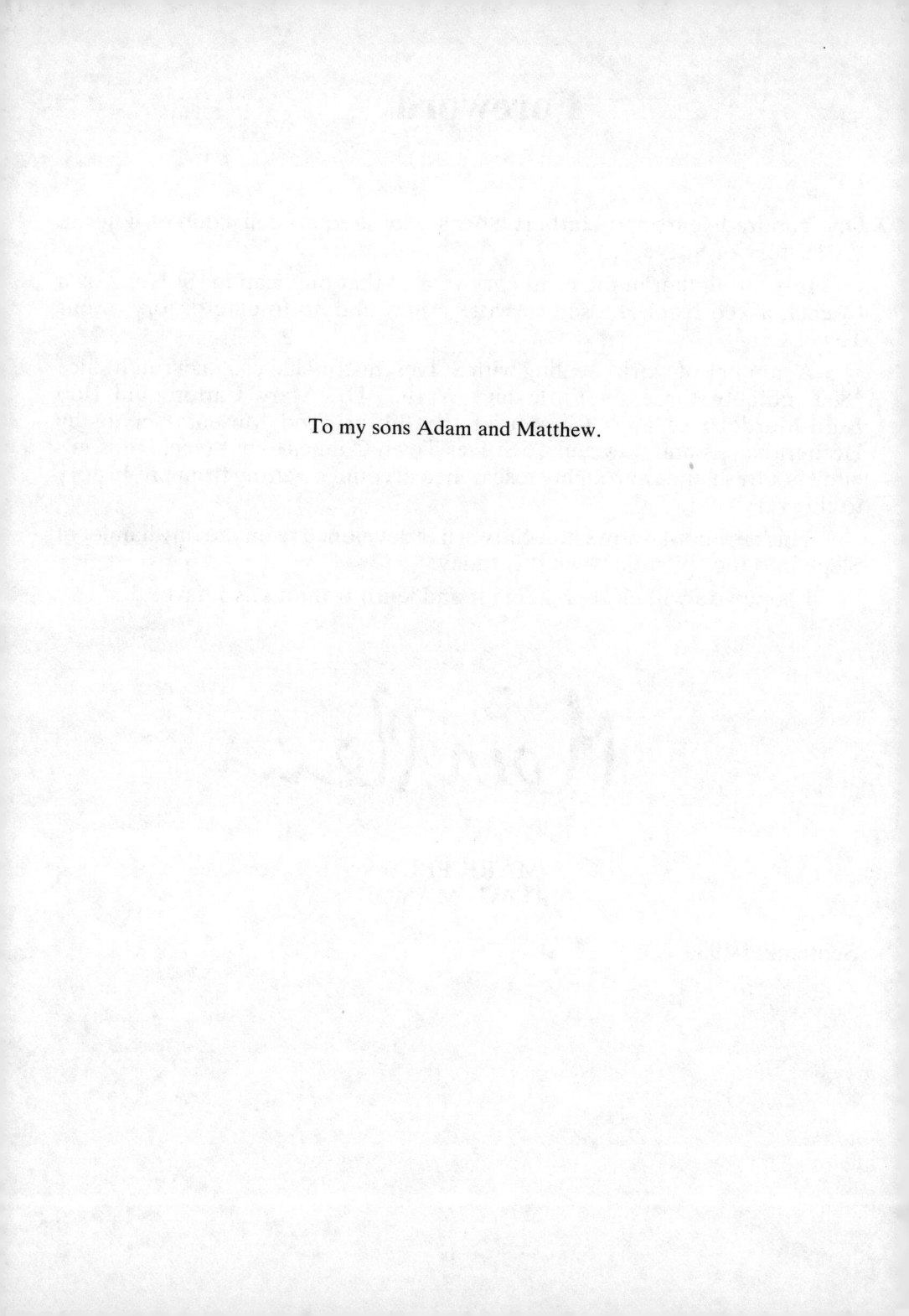

Chapter 1
A Persian Archbishop

Slepa, le Slepe, Villa Sancti Ivonis de Slepe, Strata Sancti Ivonis de Slepe, these are some of the names by which early historians referred to the first settlement established on the banks of the river Ouse which has, over the centuries, developed into the prosperous market town of St Ives. It is more likely, however, that the small band of hunters and farmers who forded the river, probably near the spot where a stone bridge now spans the Ouse, called their tiny encampment quite simply, Slepe. It would have been appropriate. Slepe was the Saxon word for muddy.

It is not known precisely when this pioneering band first arrived at Slepe, but it was probably in the fifth or sixth century. It was a turbulent era. Groups of armed men roamed the countryside raiding villages and laying waste to fields. Rural life was dangerous and uncertain. Perhaps the first arrivals at Slepe had been evicted from an earlier home in the south and were heading north in search of a remote spot in which they planned to settle down and till the soil in peace.

As they halted just a few miles from the forbidding fens, they could well have thought they had found the ideal place. They would have gazed out across the flat landscape towards the fens, wrapped almost incessantly in fog. They might have reflected that should a marauding band discover their hamlet, they could melt away into the fenland marshes and wait until the danger had passed. They would have heard how the fens were almost impenetrable in places. They might even have believed the widely held myth that those who lived among the ague-stricken swamps and marshes were web-footed.

Whatever the weary settlers had in mind, they had committed themselves to a daunting task. Huntingdonshire at that time was virtually one large forest, and it was to remain so for several centuries. The historian Leland, writing in the reign of Henry VIII, speaks of the county being extremely wooded "with the fens alive with deere." Their first job would have been to construct crude huts. Then the settlers would have had to clear some land and lay out fields to be tilled. At first they would have relied entirely on their hunters for food. There would have been no problem here. The wooded countryside was filled with wild animals.

If we are to believe the legend of St Ivo, then Slepe received a surprising visitation about a century after it had been established. One morning a tall, dignified man carrying a bishop's crozier and accompanied by two companions, girded his loins, forded the river Ouse and announced to the startled villagers that his name was Ivo and that he was a Persian archbishop. He added that he had been ordered by God to travel to Slepe where he was to make his home and preach the gospel in the surrounding area.

The non-plussed villagers appear to have accepted this surprising intelligence at its face value. They welcomed the bearded priest into their midst and carried on with their daily routine. Perhaps they reflected that it could do their spiritual future no harm at all to have so obviously an influential man of God living in their village.

For the next three centuries the inhabitants of Slepe led a blameless existence. They tilled their fields, fished the river, hunted the wild animals and probably wove cloth. The conditions under which most of them lived were wretched, but their lives were placid. As time went by some of the shrewder villagers began to acquire large amounts of land and became rich and powerful. We know that by the tenth century the Mannesonne family owned all Slepe. The manner in which one Mannesonne disposed of his possessions was to have a profound effect on the destiny of the village.

The tenth century witnessed dramatic religious developments in England. It was the century which saw the establishment of rich abbeys ruled by all-powerful abbots. Five of these great religious houses were founded in the fens. They were at Peterborough, Crowland, Thorney, Ely and, somewhat surprisingly, at Ramsey, buried deep within the cheerless fen landscape. Ramsey was not many miles away from Slepe, and perhaps the more prescient villagers might have foreseen that this proximity was going to prove highly significant. By the time Ramsey Abbey was established, Slepe had grown into a well regulated community, with bailiffs and stewards maintaining law and order and reeves dispensing justice. In 986 the then head of the Mannesonne family died and bequeathed the manor of Slepe, which included Woodhurst and Oldhurst, to Ramsey Abbey. The bequest was not straightforward and there was a dispute involving the abbey and a priest related to the Mannesonnes, but eventually the abbey acquired the manor which was at that time its largest single holding. The transition in ownership did not unduly worry the residents of the village. It made little difference to them whether their lives were controlled by a rich secular owner or a powerful religious one.

The year 1000 was to be the last during which Slepe was to doze away its time in quiet obscurity. The villagers ushered in the second millenium with church ceremonies. There was also a good deal of feasting and drinking which allowed the humbler peasants to forget briefly the uncomfortable lives they led. They could not know that in the course of the following year Bishop Ivo was to make a second unexpected visitation, on this occasion a ghostly one, and to make the name of Slepe known throughout England and even across the seas.

It was by sheer chance that a Saxon peasant, whose name has not gone down in history, inadvertently began the cult of St Ivo. One sunny morning he was tilling the fields surrounding the hamlet, when his plough struck a hard object. Pulling up his oxen, he went back to examine the spot where he had felt the impact. He dug around with his hands and came upon the lid of what appeared to be a stone coffin. The peasant ran back to the village to tell of his find and soon a group of villagers was staring down at the lid and speculating on what lay beneath it.

A concerted dig revealed the entire sarcophagus. The villagers excitedly prised open the lid and found themselves staring into the empty eye sockets of a complete human skeleton. Word spread quickly and before long the entire village was assembled at the graveside discussing the find. A bailiff and a monk soon arrived upon the scene and the remains were taken back to Slepe where they were washed and placed in the church where the villagers filed past the bones in reverence. That night the one topic of conversation in Slepe revolved around one question: whose skeleton had the villagers found?

It was not long before they were supplied with the answer. According to Goscelin, who wrote the Life of St Ivo, that night a tall, beatific figure appeared before the local smith as he lay sleeping in his hut. This man announced to the awed villager that the bones dug up in Slepe were those of the apparition now appearing before him. The figure was reputed to have proclaimed: "I am Bishop Ivo who was buried here and have lain hidden with my beloved companions until now."

He then went on to tell the smith to dig nearby the spot where the coffin had been unearthed and two more tombs would be discovered. The smith was given a final injunction to the effect that he sould retail all this to the abbot of Ramsey Abbey. Next morning the smith was so terrified he decided to put it all down to a nightmare, and said nothing. The following night the apparition again appeared before him, rebuked him for his disobedience and repeated his instructions. But once more the smith could not bring himself to tell anyone of his visitation.

On the third night the dignified old man reappeared at the smith's bedside and on this occasion spoke to him sharply. As the smith trembled with fear the visitor rapped him smartly with his crozier and said: "And you will have this sign, and will never get rid of it unless you tell what you have been ordered to." When he woke, the smith, who must by now have been on the verge of a breakdown, was wracked with pain.

The wretched man then went to the bailiff, and recounted what had happened. This official, however, turned out to be even more disbelieving than the smith had been. He dismissed the incident out of hand as a figment of his informant's imagination, and curtly remarked: "and should we translate and glorify the worthless remains of some old cobbler as those of a saint?"

According to Goscelin the bailiff was very soon to regret this churlish remark. That night it was his turn to be visited. His sleep was disturbed by a wrathful apparition who reprimanded him in no uncertain terms for his disbelief. The ghostly figure was particularly scathing about the reference to "cobbler's bones." St Ivo went on to have his revenge. He told the bailiff he had fashioned a pair of invisible leggings which would encase the official's legs until he died. At this point the sleeper awoke, stood up and promptly sat down as he felt an intense pain. The saint had indeed fastened a pair of very tight leggings to his body.

The next morning the unhappy bailiff, scarcely able to walk, made a painful journey by horse to the abbey where he told Abbot Eadnoth about his visitation. Eadnoth was naturally delighted to hear the news and hurried to Slepe accompanied by some of his monks. Having arrived at the spot where the coffin had been found, he became so excited that he seized a spade and began digging around looking for the other tombs. These were found as the apparition had predicted, and were taken to join the bones of St Ivo in the chapel. While the villagers waited for the abbot's verdict, the prelate prayed in private asking for divine guidance. Any doubts he might have had would have been removed by what he had just been told. Had not St Ivo himself identified the bones as his own? After an interval the abbot emerged to proclaim that the skeleton was indeed that of the Persian prelate and that all the remains must be taken to Ramsey Abbey where they would be suitably received. The abbot then hurried back to Ramsey to prepare for the reception.

A day or two later the remains of St Ivo together with those of his companions were solemnly borne through the countryside to Ramsey watched by crowds from all the villages in the neighbourhood. The unfortunate bailiff was left with a permanent and painful reminder that mocking saints could lead to discomfort. For years he hobbled about with chronic leg pains and for the last fifteen years of his life he was a virtual cripple. He did, however, find ultimate solace. Shortly before his death St Ivo again appeared to him, this time with an assurance that he had served his Purgatory on earth and would go straight to Heaven.

Miracles began to be reported from the outset. St Ivo's bones were carried by two monks with others following with the remains taken from the two other graves. As the procession made its way to the abbey, it was followed by a reverent crowd. Goscelin writes: "Many of the faithful also claim that during the entire journey of this joyful translation, a snow white dove flew over blessed St Ivo's remains, a miracle so widely observed that all would affirm the dove had come from heaven to favour the saint."

The procession was received at the abbey with impressive reverence and that night St Ivo made yet another visitation, this time to a monk, and asked that the abbot build a shrine in a spot accessible to all those who wanted to go and pray before the bones. The abbot immediately drew up plans for an imposing shrine, and while he was about it, decided that a second shrine should be built on the site of the find. In due course a priory was built at Slepe which, along with the original parish church at the other end of the village, dominated the small settlement. Where this priory stood is not clear, but what evidence exists suggests it was slightly east of Market Hill, somewhere in the area which now extends from the bus station to the old railway bridge.

Who was this Persian missionary? St Ivo is a shadowy figure who gleams fitfully in the flickering light of the torches which burnt night and day at the four corners of the magnificent shrine built for him by the monks of Ramsey Abbey. The only detailed account of his life and miracles is contained in an account written towards the end of the eleventh century by a Flemish monk named Goscelin. He travelled to England about 1058 and wandered the country offering to write or to re-write the histories of the great monasteries. Goscelin was a talented writer with a flair for colourful descriptive phrases.

In due course he arrived at Ramsey Abbey whose name was by now inextricably linked with St Ivo, and offered to write its history. In one respect his account is confusing. He relates the miracles in a disorganised manner and it is impossible to date many of them. Goscelin wrote in Latin, and claimed he was drawing on a Life written by abbot Andrew Withman who is known to have travelled in the Middle East where he heard the story of St Ivo who had acquired fame in Greece. Withman's writings have not survived, but we know Goscelin was a reputable historian, and there is no reason to suppose that he invented the abbot. In writing his own account, he no doubt supplemented Withman's record of miracles with the reminiscences of the older monks who would have been familiar with the entire story of St Ivo.

One of the handful of people to have read Goscelin's original manuscript and to have translated it into English is Sue Edgington. She lives in Buckden and is a senior lecturer in history and communications studies at the Huntingdonshire College. A professional historian, she is one of the world's leading authorities on the saint. In 1985 she published *The Life and Miracles of St Ivo* based on her translation of Goscelin's work.

In dealing with Goscelin we must remember that he was not writing a biography as we would define that word. He was writing hagiography. Hagiography relates to the writing of the lives of saints, and saints have always had to conform to a particular pattern. A hagiographer has to ensure that the person he is writing about conforms to this pattern, that he or she has all the qualities that people expect of a saint.

When it comes to St Ivo himself we must remember that we are going back almost a thousand years in time and we must not analyse his story with twentieth-century cynicism. Towards the end of the tenth century it was a widely held belief that the coming millenium would witness the second coming of Christ and therefore the end of the world. When these predictions were not fulfilled a mood of spiritual uncertainty gripped people. Many became prey to strange influences and a positive mania began to develop about the possession of holy relics.

The great monastic institutions led the way in this respect. They fostered a medieval obsession with bones, teeth, bits of nail clippings, snippets of hair and shreds of clothing or shrouds which could claim to have belonged to a saint. This reverence survives to some extent today, but in the eleventh century the humbler people developed an almost morbid fascination for these objects. It is not difficult to understand why this should happen. Most people lived insecure and miserable lives. Religion was one of their greatest comforts, and as they surveyed the bleak, dangerous world in which they lived, their one hope was that God would grant them a better life in the hereafter. If they could fasten on to an object known to have belonged to a saint, they could pray to it, asking the saint to intercede with God on their behalf and give them happiness after death. Saints were highly venerated and the discovery of any of their remains was a cause for great rejoicing and also for great shows of reverence.

The monks who ran the great monasteries were sensitive to this attachment their parishioners had to relics and were also acutely aware of the commercial possibilities. They competed fiercely with one another to acquire holy memorabilia. It was not uncommon for the monks of one abbey to raid a neighbouring monastery to steal relics. Not only did abbey plunder abbey, but crusaders ransacked foreign countries, notably those in the Middle East, searching for saintly hardware. Those who traded in relics could be ruthless.

This atmosphere was highly conducive to duplicity. Fakes and forgeries abounded, but this fact was irrelevant to those who believed a relic to be holy and who prayed before it.

Relics were big business. They pulled in pilgrims who in turn generated income and they bestowed fame on the shrine to which they flocked.

In the matter of relics Ramsey Abbey, which was destined to become one of the richest and most powerful religious houses in the land, was practically a pauper when the eleventh century dawned. It had the bones of two obscure Kentish princes murdered in 664, and also had on display a piece of wood said to be from Christ's cross. As most abbeys had similar pieces of wood for which identical claims were made, this meagre collection did not inspire many pilgrims to make the long journey into the fens.

The monks of Ramsey Abbey would certainly have been on the look out for more substantial and dramatic relics, and the discovery at Slepe must have been a godsend to them. Having said that, one must not assume that when they proclaimed the bones found at Slepe to be those of St Ivo, they were acting on purely venal grounds. It would be wrong to believe that fame and money were their only yardsticks. The monks who ran Ramsey Abbey were highly educated men. Some of them were men of drive, imagination and great intellectual power. They were also christians, and would surely not lightly have created an elaborate farce over a set of bones they were convinced were of no consequence. The temptation to pronounce them holy must have been strong, but it must surely be doing them an injustice to assume they did not have some grounds for believing they were confronting the mortal remains of the Persian missionary.

Those grounds existed. The monks would have known that there were records of missionaries emerging from the Middle East to preach in Europe and England. At least one of these men was reported to have crossed the channel into England. Abbot Eadnoth, as he gazed down for the first time at the skeleton unearthed in Slepe would have wondered from the outset whether he was looking upon the remains of St Ivo. His abbey was sadly lacking in spectacular holy relics. It was also competing for pilgrims with neighbouring abbeys better endowed with holy memorabilia. Could the discovery of these bones be a sign that God was showing favour to Ramsey?

Another thought would have nagged at his mind. If he was right and the bones were those of St Ivo, he would have been imperilling his own soul if he dismissed them as worthless and consigned them to an unmarked grave. Weighing all the evidence, it seems certain the abbot sincerely believed that God had bestowed a signal favour upon his abbey and that he was looking at the remains of a saintly Persian missionary. In that case his course of action was clear. The bones must be taken to Ramsey Abbey where they would be venerated. The fact that this would result in drawing pilgrims into the fens and thereby swelling the abbey's revenue would be just a bonus. It is comparatively easy to pick holes in the account of how St Ivo came to reside in Slepe. The story is woolly and raises many questions to which there are no answers. But as Sue Edgington observes: "The sheer unlikeliness of the story is the only thing that argues for a grain of truth. Why invent a Persian saint?"

Reading Sue Edgington's translation of Goscelin's manuscript, one is forced to ask the question once more: Just how much of what he was saying and doing about St Ivo did abbot Eadnoth really believe? Goscelin's Life is not a biography. It is the recital of a cult. It is significant that this cult was launched at a time when relics were the rage. Monasteries went to extreme lengths to acquire them and, having done so, did their best to see they were not seized and carried off by covetous competitors. Abbot Eadnoth would have been well aware that barely 30 years earlier the monks of Eynesbury had organised a daring raid in Cornwall and seized the bones of St Neot.

His own abbey had only the princely bones from Kent and a bit of mouldy wood. The possibility of supplementing these with the skeleton of a real saint and not only a saint but one with an exotic background, would have delighted him. This must be a sign from God. One thing is certain. The relics of St Ivo were found. They were not looted or bequeathed. In the light of what we know it seems certain the abbot was convinced he had found the bones of St

Fig. 1. St Ivo, as depicted in the icon in St Ives parish church.

Ivo. In that case any material benefits that resulted from the find were meant to be enjoyed. Who was he to look God's gift in the mouth? Two religious shrines within a few miles of each other would be certain to attract pilgrims. An intelligent man, Eadnoth might even have looked far enough ahead to imagine either Ramsey or Slepe developing into a magnet for traders and merchants.

The section in which Goscelin deals with Ivo's background is farcical and cannot be treated seriously. We read of a brother named Athanatus who lived a saintly life as a hermit in a wood. When he died his body was carried to the top of a high mountain and was honoured by a community of monks. Every month they ascended the mountain to trim his hair and pare his fingernails. Reading such rubbish one is tempted to throw Goscelin away. But after this unaccountable lapse, he reverts to being the sober historian and discusses the Ivo cult in earnest terms.

Unfortunately St Ivo's bones and those of his companions vanished after the dissolution of the monasteries in 1539. There were reports that before Henry VIII's men arrived to ransack Ramsey Abbey and the priory at Slepe the bones were smuggled away and hidden in Bodsey House, not far from the abbey. Archaeological digs have failed to locate them. Had the remains survived they could now be tested, as was the Turin shroud, by the latest radio carbon dating methods.

Sue Edgington sums up her belief when she writes: "In the end it is just not possible to tell what the monks of Ramsey found in 1001. And in the end it probably hardly matters since the growth of the cult of St Ivo does not depend on his 'reality.' He was what we might now call a media creation in an advertising campaign which eventually brought remarkable wealth and prosperity to the abbey of Ramsey and to the village of Slepe."

As soon as it was completed the priory began to draw pilgrims to the village and their numbers rapidly grew as tales of the miracles wrought at the shrine began to spread. Gradually, as the area around the priory developed and eventually swallowed up the original settlement, the burgeoning town began to be known as St Ives and not as Slepe.

Having placed all the remains in suitably grand settings, abbot Eadnoth then set about getting official recognition for his finds. He claimed that he was in possession of the bones of a saint. To get this verified was a much simpler business in the eleventh century than it was to become later on. By the thirteenth century canonisation had become a complicated business involving the Pope himself. But when St Ivo was borne in triumph to Ramsey it was only necessary to get a local bishop to investigate and to pronounce on a claim. What was more it did not have to be the diocesan bishop. Any bishop would do, and claimants naturally turned to friendly ones.

In this case abbot Eadnoth, whether he realised it or not, had pre-empted an important part of any inquiry. He was not calling for the recognition of a new saint. He was claiming he had found a ready made one. In due course the two shrines were consecrated at solemn ceremonies and the bones of St Ivo's two companions were transferred back to Slepe. Goscelin tells us: "The famous Ethelfleda was present at these gracious religious processions with a gathering of nobles. She was revered for her sermons, for her fasts and for other pious acts, and she had even founded with honour the monastery of Eynesbury and splendidly endowed it."

The countryside was already alight with tales of miracles at the Ramsey shrine, and after Slepe had received back its share of the relics, miracles were reported from there as well. Some spoke of a ray of light arched in the sky between Ramsey and Slepe and many inexplicable cures were said to have occurred at both shrines.

Sue Edgington divides the miracles into three categories – visions, retributory miracles and miracles of healing. The dove hovering over St Ivo's bier and the visitations of the saint clearly fall into the first category. So does the arched beam of light linking the two communities.

On another occasion villagers who had been "lingering agreeably over supper and drinks well into the night" suddenly saw a very bright light in the sky and reported "flashing pillars of golden light piercing the sky from the tomb of blessed St Ivo and his companions." Only a cynic would put this manifestation down to the fact that the villagers had been lingering agreeably over their drinks. The villagers were more likely to have witnessed a natural phenomenon easily explained by meteorologists today.

St Ivo had dealt swiftly with the disbelieving bailiff and the hesitant smith, and after he had been enshrined in Ramsey he continued to mete out summary justice to those who mocked or offended him. Goscelin recounts several instances of such punishment involving monks.

One was suddenly taken ill, gripped with stabbing pains and suffered "a poisonous swelling of decaying skin" because he derided the saint. Only after he had appeased St Ivo by praying and offering gifts did he recover. Another doubter who had accompanied a foreign abbot to the shrine watched his master pay his respects and then remarked to a companion that it was improper for a wise and devout man to go along with what was only the silliness of country folk. This cynic suddenly became so weak he could hardly continue his journey. Once again only retraction and piety restored him to health.

Not only men of the cloth but lay people also felt the wrath of St Ivo if they cast doubt upon the sanctity of his shrines. Goscelin chronicles one case involving a boy named Alwold. He came to Slepe with a group of pilgrims, but his aim was not to worship but to mock. While his companions were praying, Alwold placed a snow white hen on the altar as if it were hatching eggs. He then bowed in mock reverence before the altar, standing on his left leg and holding the other one in a position which made it look stunted. He then shouted the name of the saint, imploring him to cure him of his handicap. The boy intended, when he eventually put his right foot down, to cry out to the people that they had just witnessed a miracle. Instead, he found to his horror that his leg remained paralysed in the unnatural position in which he had placed it. He was never able to walk normally again.

Goscelin's final paragraph on this incident is chilling " . . . great mercy was extended to the boy, since he was not suddenly struck down by lightning for rashly provoking the Lord, or banished or dragged down to hell, but was saved by reproof in this world for eternal forgiveness."

It is possible, as Sue Edgington suggests, that this fierce defence of St Ivo's shrines illustrates an underlying lack of faith in the saint. The severity of the punishments reported to have been handed out may have silenced doubters, but it raises questions in modern minds. If the monks really believed they had found the bones of a saint, would they then have felt it necessary to instil so much terror into people?

The miracles attributed to St Ivo were by no means all vengeful. He was reported to have shown mercy to many people suffering from severe illnesses or physical deformities. A pre-condition of all these cures was faith.

Leprosy was the scourge of the Middle Ages and Goscelin records cases of sudden, totally unexpected cures. Springs flowed out of the shrines both at Ramsey and Slepe and their waters were believed to have miraculous qualities. They were said to have sprung spontaneously from the earth when the shrines were built. In fact the springs were, in all probability, underground wells found when the earth above was dug to lay the foundations of the shrines. The excavations could have released these waters.

According to Goscelin a leprous woman, her skin "itching and bristling like a hedgehog with thorny, prickling pains," had travelled far and wide going from shrine to shrine seeking a cure. Finally she came to Slepe where she washed herself in the waters of the spring, praying all the time. Shortly after these ablutions she was cured and spread news of this miracle.

One of Goscelin's reasons for emphasising that the woman had unsuccessfully visited many other shrines before arriving in Slepe was obviously to demonstrate how powerfully the

Persian bishop could intercede with God. One could equally well argue, however, that it simply showed that patients seeking cures did not think very highly of St Ivo, and only came to him in desperation as a last resort, as some patients today hawk their symptoms from one consultant to another.

It is worth pointing out that the woman's cure was not instantaneous. In the Middle Ages the term leprosy was used to include all manner of skin diseases such as those now known today as eczema, erisypelis and psoriasis. If the woman had been suffering from one of these complaints, a remission or indeed a complete cure would have been possible. Belief and faith could also have played a part. Doctors now are well aware of the importance of psychology in treating physical illnesses. Patients who trust their doctors and have confidence in the drugs they are prescribed, stand a better chance of being cured than do doubters.

Goscelin cites many cases of people cured of blindness, deafness and of crippling limb diseases. One local man was so twisted and bent he walked on all fours. After praying at St Ivo's shrine he was suddenly able to walk upright again. Abbot Eadnoth himself availed himself of the miraculous properties of the waters on his doorstep. After bathing in them he watched a nasty skin complaint clear up. Goscelin too, appears to have been a believer, for he was fortunate enough to be cured of gout. On another occasion the saint took pity on him after he had spent a sleepless night because of a raging toothache. The next morning, after he had dipped his mouth and teeth three times into the spring, his toothache vanished.

There is a colourful account of the daughter of a rich man who was holding a feast when disaster struck. The guests were enjoying themselves when the girl "was caught like a fish on a hook when she tried to swallow down a morsel of bread dissolved in her mouth. For by a hideous mischance a pin had slipped from a young servant's dress and had been folded in and cooked when the bread was made."

In the panic that ensued every possible means of getting the pin out of the girl's throat was tried without success. Then one of the guests was despatched to the shrine and came back with a phial of water. Goscelin goes on: "Suddenly when the girl drank the divine liquid the iron was dissolved and was extracted from the bottom of her throat; it came up and she had it all bloody in her mouth and spat it out."

St Ivo's chroniclers make certain that most of the miracles are witnessed by many people. A later writer on the saint describes at length the case of a woman who fell asleep in a field. While she slept, a snake stole through her open mouth and slid down into her stomach "surrounding her intestines with snakish coils." Every known remedy was again tried and was again shown to be useless. Finally the woman's family took her to Slepe. The account tells us: "There, after two or three days of fasting, vigils and prayer, she drank with very great devotion from the blessed confessor's little spring. And it was done. When the internal course flooding in gradually drenched it with holy water the snake moved more sharply than usual. As it had not found rest inside, it was vomited up, a dreadful sight of course, in front of the high altar itself, in the full view of the many people who were there at the time praying for the woman to the Lord and to St Ivo."

Goscelin also cites cases where people were "possessed by a devil." A particularly vivid account involves a Ramsey monk who went berserk one evening. He started to rave and rant, gnash his teeth and charge about biting his fellow monks. He was finally overpowered, tied up and knocked senseless by his captors with a crowbar. This would not be as brutal as it sounds. The first thing the monks would want to do once they had subdued their colleague would be to calm him down. Today if a man goes berserk he is tranquillised as soon as medical help can be obtained. In the Middle Ages a crowbar would have been as good as anything else to achieve the same purpose.

The unconscious man was then put into a large jar filled with holy water, but when he came round, undoubtedly suffering from a blinding headache, his rage was greater than it had been before. Hanging holy charms around his neck proved fruitless, and he was finally carried to St Ivo's shrine, the monks hanging on grimly to their struggling and cursing patient. As they entered the chapel leading to the shrine, the monk fell silent and then began singing a Christmas hymn. After St Ivo had been implored to intercede on his behalf, and the monk had touched the piece of linen which hung in front of the shrine, he was completely calm and rational as he prayed and gave thanks to St Ivo.

The legend of St Ivo was largely built up on the belief that he could perform miracles. To understand the awe with which the "cures" attributed to him were received, we must remember that health, and life itself, were highly insecure in the Middle Ages. We know from excavations of Anglo-Saxon burial grounds that the average age of death in Kent was 24. In Leicestershire it was 31 and in Norfolk 34. Half the population died before reaching the age of 30, and illnesses we now dismiss as trivial were killers.

The causes of disease were not understood. They were held to be punishments sent down by God. By this token, if he so felt like it, God could withdraw the disease. The complete lack of understanding of germs allowed one lot of patients to drink from waters in which another set of sufferers were soaking dreadfully diseased limbs.

The cult of St Ivo did not spread far from the local area in which he was reputed to have lived and died. There are stray references to him by subsequent historians, but these by and large appear to have been based on Goscelin's work. No other towns in England are named after him. St Ives in Cornwall is named after an entirely different saint.

We do not know when the name Slepe was last used. The name St Ives just evolved and was finally acepted. The cult of St Ivo begun by abbot Eadnoth was really promoted during the abbacy of Herbert Losinga. A Norman, he was brought to England by William Rufus and he was elected abbot of Ramsey Abbey in 1087. He remained in that position only four years before being appointed bishop of Thetford. He later went on to display remarkable administrative talents.

Herbert had already shown signs of this talent at Ramsey. He encouraged Goscelin to write his Life of the saint, and was extremely active in promoting Slepe as a centre for pilgrims and in encouraging the cult of the saint for all it was worth. By publicising the miracles through Goscelin's writings he drew more and more pilgrims to Slepe and the tiny settlement which had been started by the wandering Saxons four or five centuries earlier lost its anonymity and began to become famous.

The monks, realising the need for good communications, were the first to build a primitive bridge across the river in the early part of the twelfth century. Henry I set the seal on St Ives' fame when he granted it a charter to hold an eight-day annual Easter fair in 1110.

Ramsey Abbey owed the start of its climb to great wealth partly to Slepe and the discovery of a stone coffin. Slepe in turn owed its rise to fame largely to the foresight and marketing skill of the abbots of the monastery. Had the bones which became the foundation of the cult been discovered in another village not under the rule of Ramsey Abbey, their fate could have been very different. Had they been unearthed, say at Spaldwick, it is possible they could have been quietly re-interred. In that case there would have been no St Ivo, who is listed in the *Oxford Dictionary of Saints*, the legend of the saint would not have been born, there would never have been a Slepe Priory, and the town now called St Ives might very well be known today as Slepe.

Chapter 2
Prehistoric St Ives

Our knowledge of St Ivo comes from the book that Goscelin wrote 900 years ago, which has luckily survived to the present day. Discovering the past from written evidence is what "history" is all about. But to go further back in time, and to find out what St Ives was like before there were any written records – that is, in "pre-historic" times – we have to use other techniques.

It is surprising just how much we can find out from unwritten evidence. Archaeologists can study the remains left by people of previous ages, and can use them to form some idea of how they lived thousands of years ago. And other specialists can examine the remains of extinct animals found in the gravels of the Ouse valley, laid down during the last 130,000 years, or look at the fossils of even earlier creatures buried deep in the local bedrock, which was formed about 160 million years ago. It may seem unbelievable that corals and sea urchins and plesiosaurs once lived in the town we now call St Ives, that Mammoths roamed here or that Elephants lived at nearby Fenstanton, and Hippopotamus wallowed at Huntingdon. But the remains of all these animals have been found in or near St Ives, and can be seen in the town's Norris Museum. And by a careful study of these remains, it is possible to build up a very detailed picture of what life in St Ives was like, millions upon millions of years ago.

The first light of dawn revealed an extensive sea with a fairly heavy swell whipped up by oceanic winds from the south. The surface was broken by the long neck of a plesiosaur, which then promptly dived in search of fish. In the distance ichthyosaurs could be seen porpoising. Apart from the far-off shore of a large island to the east, there was no sight of land, although a great continent lay over the horizon to the west.

This would have been the scene confronting a time traveller searching for the site of St Ives at the time that the geological deposit which underpins the area, the Oxford Clay, was laid down. This stratum, which runs diagonally across England, started its life as mud at the bottom of a sea about 160 million years ago in the late part of the Jurassic Period, 215–145 million years ago.

At that time the geography of the world was very different from today's, as, with sea floor spreading and continental drift, the distribution of land and sea would have been unrecognisable. There were two supercontinents, Laurasia, combining North America, Europe and northern and central Asia, and Gondwanaland, joining together the southern continents and India. They were divided from each other by a long ocean known to geologists as the Tethys.

The waters of this ocean frequently flooded the margins of the continents and in Oxford Clay times much of England, then lying somewhat closer to the Equator, was under water in a seaway that often connected Tethys with the completely ice-free Arctic Ocean and split Laurasia in two. This sea possessed a rich fauna as is evidenced by the fossil record of the area. The dominant invertebrates were the ammonites, tentacled creatures with their bodies encased in spiral shells not unlike that of the living *Nautilus* of tropical seas; belemnites, squid-like animals with long bullet-shaped guards or internal shells, were also prominent.

There was a wide variety of fishes, most of them belonging to families which have long since disappeared. Sharks, large and small, were however similar to their living descendants. The invertebrates and fishes provided the prey for the animals at the top of the food chain, the

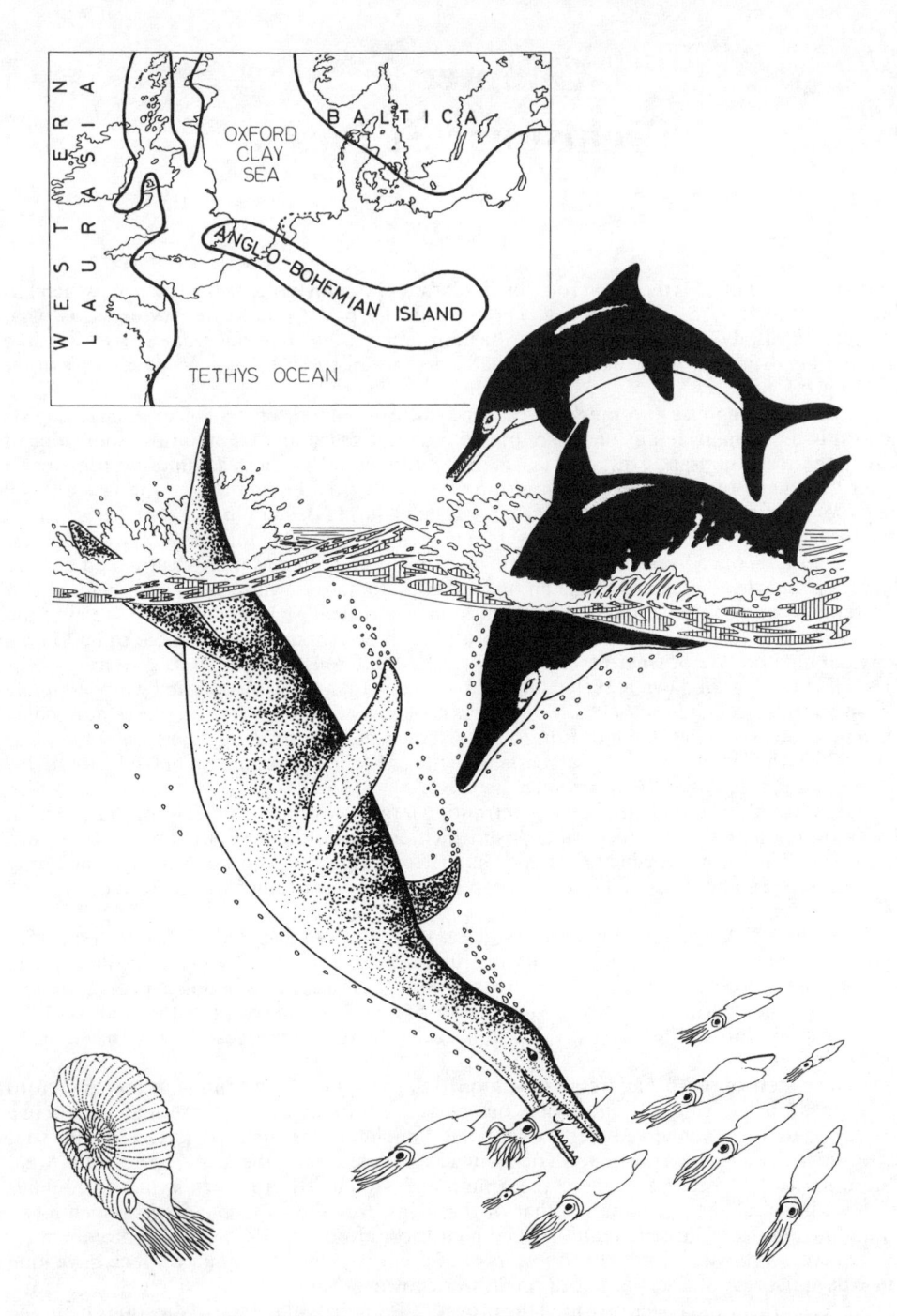

Fig. 2. St Ives 160 million years ago: a short-necked plesiosaur and a pair of ichthyosaurs dive to feed on a shoal of belemnites and an ammonite.

marine reptiles. Among them we find sea-going crocodiles, such as *Metriorhynchus*, plesiosaurs, some long necked (*Cryptocleidus*) and some short (*Peloneustes*), and the porpoise-like ichthyosaurs, the largest of which was *Ophthalmosaurus*. All these animals have left their remains in deposits in and around St Ives. On land, some of the mightiest dinosaurs that ever existed dominated terrestrial life.

As the Jurassic drew to a close, to be succeeded by the Cretaceous Period, 145–66 million years ago, the sea withdrew from most of Britain, only to return even more extensively around 100 million years ago, and to remain for more than 30 million years. It was in the waters of the Great Chalk Sea that the remains of calcareous algae formed a white ooze on the seabed which eventually became the chalk deposits of southern England. At one time these chalk strata lay over the Oxford Clay in Huntingdonshire, but earth movements, related to the raising of the Alps about 25 million years ago, led to extensive folding of strata and the removal, through erosion, of much of the chalk and later cover.

The end of the Cretaceous and with it the Mesozoic Era, about 66 million years ago, witnessed an ecological disaster on a gigantic scale. Nearly three quarters of all species then living died out, including all the dinosaurs, the great marine reptiles and the ammonites; the belemnites were to follow them shortly afterwards. Scientists still argue about whether this was the result of the Earth being hit by a comet or colossal meteorite, or a massive increase in vulcanism or because of other factors.

Whatever the reason, the result was clear – a fairly empty world in which the survivors could evolve to fill the niches which had become vacant. Mammals, including our own remote ancestors, had remained small, mainly nocturnal creatures throughout the long reign of the dinosaurs. Now was their chance and they met the challenge, evolving into everything from mice to elephants, giraffes to whales and lions to monkeys, apes and ultimately our own species. Birds, themselves the descendants of light running carnivorous dinosaurs, also flourished.

The age of mammals, the Cenozoic Era, in which we still live, saw in its early stages the final opening of the North Atlantic and the gradual withdrawal of the sea to the south-east, leaving the Reading and Woolwich Beds and the London Clay in its wake. Britain became dry land joined to the Continent and the build up of the Alps, caused by Africa's steady move north and the obliteration of Tethys, produced the Chilterns and the North and South Downs and gave the final moulding to the country before the onset of the Ice Ages.

Five million years ago the climate of the Earth grew noticeably cooler and the Pleistocene Epoch, beginning just under two million years ago, saw a series of very cold periods in which ice caps advanced from high into middle latitudes, interspersed with warmer intervals such as the one in which we are now living. Each complete cycle lasted about 120,000 years, the earlier glaciations being somewhat less severe than those of the last half-million years, when ice sheets, a mile or more thick, ground their way south, completely covering the St Ives area and sweeping away most superficial geological deposits.

The ice advance did not stop until it had reached the hills which now separate inner London from its northern suburbs. The Thames, which had formerly flowed through the Vale of St Albans in the direction of Harwich, was blocked and forced to carve a channel for itself further south which it still uses.

The ice sheet of the penultimate or Wolstonian glaciation probably covered this region but the last glaciation stopped well short of it, leaving a record of the warm interglacial and the succeeding cold periods in the gravels of the Great Ouse.

The Wolstonian glaciation ended abruptly 128,000 years ago. This date and others which mark climatic changes are based on a recent study of climatic variations evidenced by pollen records over the last 140,000 years. The last or Ipswichian interglacial, during which temperatures were, on average, 2°C higher than today's, lasted from 128,000 down to 112,000 years ago, when the climate experienced a marked cooling.

The Ouse valley supported a rich mammalian fauna. Many species, still native to this country such as the Red and Fallow Deer, were to be found. Others, like the Lion and the Hyena, now live only in warmer climates. The Hippopotamus could be seen wallowing in the Ouse. Two species, now extinct, were prominent, the Narrow-nosed Rhinoceros (*Didermocerus hemitoechus*), a close relation of the still living but extremely rare two-horned Sumatran Rhinoceros (*D. sumatrensis*) and the enormous Straight-tusked Elephant (*Palaeoloxodon namadicus*), which ranged over temperate Eurasia from Portugal to Japan.

As the full interglacial came to an end around 112,000 years ago, it ushered in a colder period, the Devensian, which lasted for 100,000 years. The earlier part saw two cold periods, known as stadials, each followed by somewhat warmer interstadials, the latter about 100,000 and 80,000 years ago.

The warmth-loving animals disappeared gradually and there was clearly a considerable amount of coming and going as the climate alternately ameliorated and worsened. There is evidence of a typical interglacial fauna in Wales as late as 81,000 years ago, and it is reasonable to assume that the same held good for Huntingdonshire. The real severity of an ice age was just ahead, as by 72,000 years ago the ice sheets were advancing.

They slackened a bit about 60,000 years ago, leading to an interstadial lasting 30,000 years which was, nonetheless, extremely cold, to be followed by the final and most severe ice advance which reached its maximum extent about 18,000 years ago. The ice sheet stretched as far south as the Kings Lynn area and southern England became tundra similar to that in northern Siberia, Alaska and Canada today.

Vast quantities of water were locked up in ice sheets, causing the sea level to drop to the 100 m level and leaving the North Sea, English Channel and Irish Sea as dry land. Owing to the low level of the sea, rivers, including the Great Ouse, cut deeply into the gravel beds and ran more swiftly.

The change in the climate saw a great change in the animal life. With tundra conditions prevailing locally for most of the last 60,000 years of the Pleistocene, the Reindeer and Muskox became common and the Woolly Mammoth (*Mammuthus primigenius*) and the Woolly Rhinoceros (*Coelodonta antiquitatis*) moved into the area. It is probable that, at the height of the glaciation, this fauna moved south but, for much of the long cold interstadial, these animals featured prominently on the scene. As the ice-sheet retreated, so also did the species but the Mammoth was still present in Shropshire 12,800 years ago. It appears to have become completely extinct about 11,000 years ago for reasons which are still unclear. The Woolly Rhinoceros by then was already extinct.

Man had appeared in Europe about 500,000 years ago from his original African home. Early hand axes of the Acheulian industry have survived in Huntingdonshire, apparently overridden by ice sheets, and may date back 400,000 years. A wealth of flint tools of the more sophisticated Levalloisian industry survive from the Ipswichian interglacial and the early years of the Devensian. This later industry was probably the work of an early strain of Neandertal Man. The last half of the Devensian produced conditions in southern England which were doubtless too severe for tolerable human existence.

Conditions in southern Europe were far from ideal at the time but the Neandertals seemed to thrive there until they were replaced by Modern Man some time between 35,000 and 30,000 years ago. These newcomers proved themselves more efficient toolmakers than the Neandertals and, as the years rolled by, accomplished artists on cave walls as well. It was not, however, until the final disappearance of the ice that Britain began to attract these resourceful ancestors of ours.

As the ice sheets retreated and melted, there was a sudden improvement in the climate at 10,700 years ago, 400 years before the date normally taken to mark the transition from the Pleistocene to the Holocene (or Recent) Epoch (8300 B.C.). Vast quantities of water were returned to the sea, which rose and began to fill the basins of the North Sea and the English

Fig. 3. St Ives 120,000 years ago (*above*): Straight-tusked Elephant, Rhinoceros, Hippopotamus, Lion cubs and Hyena; and St Ives 35,000 years ago (*below*), with Mammoth, Woolly Rhinoceros and Reindeer.

Channel, although for centuries Britain remained connected with the Continent by a low-lying marshy plain across the southern part of the North Sea. The Rivers Great Ouse and Nene joined and travelled north to link up with the Humber before emptying into the sea. The Thames, its waters flowing through a large lake where the Black Deep now lies, was for a time a tributary of the Rhine.

Around 6500 B.C. the sea finally broke through at the Straits of Dover and Britain became an island. With the warmer climate tundra gave way to extensive forest. The Fenland area remained heavily wooded until about 4000–3000 B.C., when the rising sea flooded much of the basin, at least half-way up to the site of Earith, drowning the forests in the process and leaving the bog oaks and peat as evidence of their former existence. Gradually sediment brought down by the rivers filled the basin, pushed back the shore line and created the marshes which characterised the Fens until they were systematically drained.

This is, however, to run ahead of man's occupation of this area. Following the retreat of the ice, Britain, still joined by land to Europe, lay open to bands of hunter-gatherers. They were not slow in exploiting their opportunity.

St Ives and Huntingdonshire must have been a wild and beautiful Garden of Eden for those first settlers after the Ice Ages. As the climate improved, great forests grew up in the west of the county, with oak trees 90 feet tall. To the east, peat was gradually choking the Fens. In between the two, the light gravel soils of the Ouse valley formed a strip of well-drained, less thickly wooded country, where the settlers could make their homes.

From the valley they could go out in all directions in their quest for food. The forest harboured wild boar, a ferocious quarry but good eating. The Fens teemed with fish and wildfowl, and had many edible plants. Even in the present century, hungry Fen schoolchildren knew some types of rush had roots that could be pulled up and eaten raw. In the open country between forest and fen roamed wild oxen, elk and deer. Squirrels, beaver and otter could be hunted for their fur. All in all, there was much to tempt people to make the trek across the lowlands that now lie at the bottom of the North Sea, to come to this area.

Some time between 4000 and 3500 B.C., this way of life began to change. It is then that we find the first evidence that Huntingdonshire people were not just hunting for their food, but starting to farm it as well. The techniques of the early farmers were crude. They cut clearings in the forest by felling trees with their stone axes. Then they burned the fallen timber to leave small plots among the trees, rich in wood ash. Crops were grown for a few years until the soil was exhausted, then new clearings were made, and livestock was grazed on the old plots. Once again the Ouse valley was an important area, as the early farmers moved into the edges of the forest from the open ground along the river. Two of their stone axes have been found at Houghton, just upstream from St Ives.

Around 2000 B.C., something else happened that involved the Ouse. Boats came upstream, manned by the mysterious invaders known to archaeologists as the Beaker People. They are named after their fine pottery drinking cups, the best pottery to be seen in this country until the arrival of the Romans 2000 years later, and we know that they used the Ouse as one of their routes into England because Beakers have been found at regular intervals along its banks, including two at Houghton. The Beaker People brought to this country the knowledge of how to work bronze, instead of the flint that had been used to make tools and weapons before. A bronze spearhead has been found buried beside Bridge Street in St Ives, and a bronze dagger has been dredged from the river below St Ives Staunch.

About 650 B.C. iron began to replace bronze. In the Iron Age too, archaeological finds have shown that St Ives continued to be inhabited. In A.D. 43 came a more dramatic change, with the invasion of Britain by the Romans. The invading armies passed close to St Ives, building a fort to guard the ford across the Ouse at Godmanchester, about five miles upstream. But when the legions marched north to continue their conquest of Britain, the tribes they left behind took their revenge. In A.D. 60–61 the Iceni tribe of East Anglia rose in rebellion under their queen Boudicca, or Boadicea, and fell on the Roman settlers who had moved into England behind the armies. Godmanchester was burned to the ground, and it may be that there were Roman settlers in St Ives who also suffered the Iceni's vengeance. Certainly a small first-century settlement here was using pottery copied from Roman wares – the sherds were found during a dig in Priory Road in 1981.

The Romans' suppression of the Iceni was as brutal as the rising itself had been. Afterwards, the area enjoyed an interval of peace, protected behind the shield of Hadrian's Wall and the Roman army. Godmanchester rose from the ashes to become an important town, while around it the peaceful countryside was dotted with villas. There was one of these prosperous farmhouses at St Ives, and plenty of others in the country round. The standard of living enjoyed by their owners can be judged from local finds of Roman objects, such as the magnificent pewter dish, nearly two feet across, that was dredged from the river near St Ives and is on display at the Norris Museum. Prosperous Romans buried their dead in stone coffins, and the St Ives villa stood very close to where St Ivo's Priory later stood – could it be that the skeleton the Saxon ploughman found was only that of the former owner of the villa?

In any case, the Roman peace was short-lived. About A.D. 300 Godmanchester was burned again, probably by Saxon raiders coming up from the North Sea. The nearby villas, including that at St Ives, probably suffered a similar destruction. There was no dramatic end to Roman rule in Britain – Godmanchester was rebuilt, and continued a feeble existence for many years afterwards – but the complicated structure of Imperial society slowly fell apart. Farmers found that the army could no longer protect them and the dwindling towns no longer provided a market for their produce. Central power failed, and the warrior band just down the road became more important than the Governor in London, or the Emperor in distant Constantinople. It was in these conditions that the first settlers came to Slepe, and the story of the present town of St Ives began.

Chapter 3
The Black Monks

In the year when Slepe was catapulted into the limelight by an obscure, many might say questionable Persian archbishop, the village, together with the neighbouring hamlets of Woodhurst and Oldhurst, was owned by the black-robed, cowled monks of the Benedictine order at Ramsey Abbey. The mitred abbot of that great religious house ruled Slepe, and his rule was absolute.

The Benedictines are said to be the oldest order of monks. They get their name from St Benedict, a native of Nursia in the Dukedom of Spoleto in Italy. The form and colour of their habit was at first left to the discretion of individual abbots, but subsequently it was laid down that they should wear a loose gown of black reaching down to the heels, with a hood and a scapulary. Under this they were to wear another gown of white flannel. Their legs were booted. Because of the colour of their habit they became known as the Black Monks. As the peasants of Slepe, slightly bemused by their sudden fame, tilled their fields and went about their business, they were acutely aware that at any moment an edict issued from the fens could have a profound effect upon their lives.

Ramsey Abbey was founded in 969 and in time became one of the richest and most powerful in the country. Its abbots had immense influence and were feared equally by commoners and great nobles. Even royalty did not lightly cross the abbot who ruled Ramsey. The abbey had its chronicler more than 800 years ago in the person of one of its more studious monks. He probably had resort to ancient manuscripts, and his account can be seen in the Bodleian Library in Oxford. The Chronicles were studied in the last century by John Wise, a vicar of Ramsey Church and W. Mackbeth Noble, one of his curates, who based their book, *Ramsey Abbey, Its Rise and Fall*, on them.

The town of Ramsey stands in a district once known as the holy land of England: "there were Ely, Ramsey, Crowland, Thorney and Peterborough with their succursal cells". Looking back one can appreciate the extent of man's technical progress and how that progress has converted what were once bogs, meres and fens into some of the most fertile acres in the country. The fens at the time when the abbey was being founded were an uninviting area of fog shrouded marshes where agues were rife and with just one road connecting them with the rest of the country.

Yet it was in this unlikely setting in which Hereward the Wake was to make a last-ditch defiance of the Normans, that it was decided to found a great monastery. As the chronicler recalls: "St Benedict's Rule and Order was not by him instituted for cities, towns and castles, but for places remote from concourse of people, and in poverty, for the monks thereof to live by their hard labour and so as to be truly monks by his rule". Later abbots tended to give only cursory recognition to the "and in poverty" clause, but there can be no doubt that the original founders did not set themselves up in luxury.

Many eminent writers have left their impressions of what life was like in the fens in the centuries preceding the dedication of Ramsey Abbey. In the seventh century a monk named Guthlac, who lived in a monastery in Derbyshire, decided he wanted to live a more secluded life. Having heard of the fens he decided that he would go there and arrived by boat at an island he calls "Crulande". He paints a deplorable picture of the conditions he found. "For by the inundations and overflowing of rivers, the water standing upon the level ground maketh a deep lake, and so rendereth it uninhabitable, excepting in some places which God of purpose raised (as may be thought) to be habitations for his servants".

The monk continues: "For in such places within the fens do they (holy men) and many others beside dwell . . . places to which there is no access but by navigable vessels, except unto Ramsey, by a causey (causeway) raised with much labour on the one side thereof". Guthlac's readers are next treated to a horrifying account of: "a hideous fen of huge bigness oftentimes clouded with moist and dark vapours which, beginning at the banks of the river Gronte (Granta) extends itself from the south to the north, even to the sea". Guthlac also talks alarmingly about "apparitions of devils", the ones sighted in Crulande being: "devils of monstrous shapes (which) are, we think, resolveable into hallucinations caused by periodical fever attendant upon fen ague".

Daniel Defoe, the author of *Robinson Crusoe*, paints a no less ugly portrait. In his *Tour through Britain* he writes: "As we ascended westward we saw the fen country on our right almost covered with water like a sea. The Michaelmas rains having been very great that year, sent down vast floods from the upland counties, and those fens being the sink of no less than twelve counties, they are often overflowed.

"As these fens appeared overwhelmed with water, I observed that they, generally at the latter part of the year, appear almost covered with fogs, so that when the Downs and higher grounds of the adjacent country glistered with the beams of the sun, the Isle of Ely seemed wrapped up in mist and darkness, so that nothing else could be discovered but now and then the cupola of Ely Minster".

Defoe went on to express sorrow for the inhabitants of such a place where they "had no other breath to draw than what must be mixed with the choking vapours which spread all over the country". Yet he recorded with bewilderment that people somehow contrived to live to old age and, being born under such loathsome conditions, made light of incessant agues.

Lord Macaulay in his *History of England* also felt impelled to leave for posterity his thoughts on the counties between Cambridge and the Wash when he wrote in the middle of the nineteenth century. He speaks of: "a vast and desolate fen saturated with all the moisture of thirteen counties, and overhung during the greater part of the year by a low grey mist above which rose, visible many miles, the magnificent tower of Ely".

The great historian was less kind than Defoe when he came to talk about fenmen, referring to them as "a half savage population, known by the name of breedlings, who lead an amphibious life, sometimes wading, sometimes rowing, from one islet of firm ground to the other". One would imagine that such a detestable region could only be improved upon, but when the fens began to be drained, a breed of writers appeared who regretted the reclamation of the land and the improvement this brought, and sighed for the old days of what they liked to describe as the poetry and beauty of the old, untouched swamps and marshes.

Charles Kingsley, the author of *The Water Babies*, was one of these nostalgic writers. In a magazine article he wrote in 1867, he agrees it was right for the fens to have been transformed from a virtual waste into fertile farmland. At the same time he cannot resist an imaginative description of: "the shining meres, the strange and gaudy insects, the wild nature, the mystery, the majesty – for mystery and majesty there were – which haunted the deep fens for many a hundred years".

He goes on to observe that the old, virtually unexplored fens had a certain regal grandeur, and talks of dark green alders and pale green reeds amidst which "the coot clanked and the bittern boomed, and the sedge bird, not content with its own sweet song, mocked the notes of all the other birds around while high overhead hung motionless hawk beyond hawk, buzzard beyond buzzard, kite beyond kite as far as the eye could see". By now almost carried away by his prose, Kingsley talks of listening silently to "all the bells of Cambridge, and all the hounds of Cottesmore . . . while triumphant above all, sounded the wild whistle of the curlew and the trumpet note of the great wild swan". Modern ecologists, deep into pesticides and the ozone layer, would have difficulty in matching these lines that Kingsley turned out in memory of Guthlac's fens. Kingsley did draw some comfort, however, from the fact that wheat and mutton had replaced typhus and ague. He also expressed the pious hope that there would be no more "brandy drinking and opium eating and that children will live and not die". If Guthlac, Defoe and Macaulay were precise, one can well imagine fen dwellers having a tendency to turn to liquor or drugs, and the infant mortality rate must have been appalling.

Kingsley was very puzzled by the fact that despite conditions in the fens before drainage, some people did live to a ripe age. He seemed to think this was because anyone who survived his early years was apt to have a remarkable constitution.

The Ramsey chronicler gives a geographical description of the island in the tenth century and says it was the fairest of all the "Fenny Islands". It was only accessible from the west and was severed from the mainland by deep quagmires at first reached only by boat but later by a causeway.

The island was two miles long and a little less wide and was hemmed in by trees, reeds and bulrushes. The land appeared fertile as it produced corn, and the streams surrounding the island abounded with fish, eels and wildfowl. There were apparently pike of "extraordinary bigness". The chronicler says the name Ramsey comes from two Saxon words, Ram and Eie or Eye, the latter meaning island, hence Ram's Island. There was a legend that many years ago a ram had been feeding in the summer near the island and wandered on to it. He stayed for too long and when the autumn set in, he was stranded at Ramsey until the following spring before he could walk over the bogs.

The abbey was dedicated to St Benedict from its inception and was founded when that order was being fostered on English people by King Edgar, supported by archbishops Odo and Dunstan of Canterbury, Oswald, archbishop of York and by many influential families. One very conspicuous man was Duke Ailwin of East Anglia who was said to have royal origins. Odo and Dunstan are favourably mentioned in the Chronicle, but had little to do with the abbey's foundation. Ailwin and Oswald were the principal founders, while King Edgar was a notable benefactor.

He is mentioned time and again by the chronicler. He greatly favoured the monastic system and is said to have built or restored no fewer than twelve such religious houses. The king gave Ramsey gifts of land and churches and such powerful rights that the abbots became in effect absolute rulers within their domain. The liberties which Edgar bestowed were confirmed by various royal charters. Oswald and Odo were both Danish by origin.

It was Oswald who convinced Ailwin to build a monastery on land he owned to atone for his sins. Ailwin said he had hereditary land at Ramsey which would be suitable as it was cut off by marshes, but, where it had been cleared, was fertile. He had already built a small wooden cell there where three holy men lived "having renounced all the sinful lusts of the flesh and earnestly desiring to learn the rule of monastic discipline if they had anyone to teach them". Oswald promised to send Ailwin twelve monks from another monastery and this offer was accepted. The two men travelled to Ramsey, and when Oswald saw the location of the primitive chapel he is recorded to have exclaimed: "here is a second Elysium, provided from eternity for those destined for the highest place in Paradise".

In 969 serious work started on a more ambitious building than the one Ailwin had constructed. The plan of the new monastery was a cross with side aisles and the building was to be adorned with two towers, one at the west front and the other at the intersection of the cross, in other words in cruciform shape.

On November sixth 974 the completed church, which had deep foundations because of the dampness of the fen soil, was solemnly dedicated by Oswald to the guardianship of the Virgin of Virgins and to the name of St Benedict. While building was still going on the number of monks was increased and schools were established, but there was one thing lacking. In those days relics were much sought after, and the newly dedicated abbey was lacking in this respect. According to the Chronicle Ailwin had the bones of two Kentish princes who had been murdered and buried near a country house he owned and, as the relics were reported to have shown signs of the holiness of the princes while they were alive, Ailwin had them disinterred and reburied at Ramsey.

William of Malmesbury records that the princes were cousins of Egbert, king of Kent, who reigned between 664 and 673. The king feared the princes might be troublesome and had them murdered. After the bones had been reinterred at Ramsey, the chronicler speaks of many miracles occurring in response to prayers offered up by visitors to the abbey.

Only a few years after the abbey had been built, the treacherous, oozy soil on which it stood began causing problems. In the reign of Ethelred II, 979–1016, a crack opened up in the central tower, threatening the complete destruction of the abbey. The scared monks informed Ailwin who at that time was probably living at Upwood. He immediately went to Ramsey and asked the opinion of workmen who blamed insecure foundations for the trouble and advised that the whole building be taken down.

Oswald, ageing by now and living at York, was informed. He declared that "all faintheartedness must be set aside, strength vigorously used, the shaken building must be taken down and in confidence of merit which will follow, a deeper foundation must be dug . . . in short the whole building must be restored on a better foundation to the glory of God".

Ailwin, by now old and infirm, ordered work to begin and to be completed "before approaching death cuts me off, now tottering with age". When the work was completed and a more secure edifice stood upon the uncertain land, the duke ordered that a tablet be sited in front of the high altar and be dedicated to the glory of God and St Benedict. The tablet was adorned with plates of solid silver, and also with precious stones. The duke also gave £30 for the making of copper pipes for an organ.

The founders of the abbey were now growing increasingly old and the chronicler records dreams and portents foreshadowing their deaths. A brother in his sleep saw both towers of the abbey crashing, and two monks, sleeping at some distance from the monastery, one night heard a great sound as though the church had been struck by lightning. Shortly afterwards news came that Oswald had died. Ailwin himself, according to the chronicler, was filled with the certainty that his death could not long be delayed.

Assembling his family, his friends and the monks around him he declared: "old age, diminishing the strength of a feeble and crooked body, wholly takes away my wish of remaining here. The gracefulness of my once comely form is destroyed by wrinkles; the testy cough, by its frequent stinging, tires my breast; my complexion is pale, my scent is less acute than formerly; what I taste relishes less; scarcely can I support my tottering steps with a staff; hardly will my trembling hands hold anything fast . . . it is pleasant to die when life is found to be so irksome". Not long after this graphic description of advanced old age, Ailwin died and was buried at Ramsey.

The duke had conferred on his monastery the whole of the island of Ramsey, he also bequeathed to the abbey many estates and valuable gifts. For twenty years after its foundation Oswald himself had been the nominal abbot of Ramsey Abbey, though the day to day running of the monastery had been entrusted to two priors. On Oswald's death Eadnoth – "a model of zeal and industry" – became the first elected abbot. When Duke Ailwin died, Eadnoth and after him succeeding abbots, set about using their newly acquired wealth to extend their influence. They bought extensive properties and acquired such prosperity that the abbey became known as Ramsey the Rich. By this time it was no longer lacking in crowd-pulling relics. Eadnoth had been in control when the abbey came into possession of the bones of St Ivo. As the years went by the abbots began to exercise almost regal powers.

By the end of the eleventh century their lives were well organised and the monks led routine daily lives. Each had his specific duties to perform, tilling the fields and cultivating the gardens. The older monks spent hours in contemplation or in the enormous library which was gradually built up, reading religious books and studying the lives of the saints. At least twice a day on weekdays there were periods of prayer and meditation in the church.

During the abbacy of Ailwin statutes were drawn up setting out the rules of the household which by now numbered about 80 monks. These statutes describe a regime that was simple but by no means harsh. They show that the staple articles of diet were bread, cheese, bacon, beef and mutton as well as eggs, beans and honey. Butter and poultry were added to the refectory table on feast days.

Monasteries in those days were the homes of bookworms, architects, artisans, doctors and schoolmasters. Early writers are divided when it comes to assessing whether these religious institutions were influences for good or evil. Many writers laud the work done by the monks, but some have reservations. At least one speaks of "many humble and righteous servants of God", but adds that we should not forget that the abbeys also housed "swarms of lazy, sensual, unlettered drones".

Ramsey enjoyed a reputation as "a bright lamp of learning", and its chronicle was the source upon which the historian E. W. Brayley drew when he wrote: "many of the abbots and monks of Ramsey Abbey were men of considerable talents and learning, to which, doubtless, the school established within the walls of the abbey, and almost coeval with its foundation, greatly contributed". Brayley notes that Ramsey boasted a famous library which included Hebrew books, a rarity in those days. Jews had first been permitted to cross over from Normandy into England by William the Conqueror and had set up synagogues. But in the reign of Edward I their properties had been confiscated and the Jews themselves banished. There had been synagogues at Huntingdon and Stamford and all their property came under the hammer.

A Ramsey monk, Gregory of Huntingdon, who had been studying Hebrew but who had been handicapped by the lack of books in that language, went to the sale with plenty of money supplied by his abbot. The books Gregory acquired at the sale became the basis of a collection which later abbots built up.

The monks of the fens are also credited by some scholars for being the cradle of classic modern English. It is claimed the black monks fused together the various dialects which prevailed in medieval England into a language, a vehicle of thought for a great nation. In his *Sources of Standard English*, T. L. Kingston Oliphant writes: "it may seem strange that England's now standard speech should have sprung up, not at Edward the First's court, but in cloisters on the Nene and Welland. In no part of England, perhaps, was there such a cluster of monastic institutions within the same limits, as in the fens, none that could enjoy such seclusion. Here men had the leisure and opportunity to think and to write. The Saxon monasteries, too, were the chief, or perhaps the only schools for education, and they very early obtained certain privileges on that very account". Ramsey was the richest of the fenland abbeys, but probably because it was so remote and inaccessible, Peterborough became more famous nationally and was converted into a bishopric.

After Ailwin's death the monks met and chose Eadnoth to be their abbot, the first elected abbot of Ramsey Abbey. The fourth abbot, Ethelstan, held the abbacy for 23 years until 1043 when he was brutally murdered by a man he had rescued from destitution. During his tenure of office King Canute began building a nunnery at Ramsey with Treasury money, but the idea was abandoned and the building never completed. The chronicler notes discreetly "it being prudently considered that disadvantages might arise from the vicinity of the two sexes". It was also during Canute's reign that the remains of St Felix were added to the abbey's collection of relics.

Felix was a Burgundian monk who came to England in 630 and became Bishop of Dunwich in Suffolk. His remains had been buried in his cathedral city, but for some reason they were transferred to Soham in Cambridgeshire and from there to Ramsey. A group of monks from Ely tried to intercept the procession carrying Felix's bones to Ramsey but were beaten off after a fierce scuffle among the marshes. During the abbacy of Walter, the eleventh abbot, the monks had a hard time. The abbey was attacked and its inhabitants expelled by Geoffrey de Mandeville, one of the most lawless and turbulent of King Stephen's noblemen. He headed a rebellion against the king, sacked Cambridge and looted its churches. He then turned his attention to Ramsey Abbey. He devastated a large area of the fens and, not content with stripping the abbey and expelling the monks, he installed his own men and used the monastery as a garrison. He was finally defeated in a battle with the king's men and was killed, allowing the monks to return and start making good their oppressor's depredations.

In time the monasteries began to be regarded with increasing disfavour. Kings coveted their revenues and nobles were jealous of the supremacy of abbots. Power led to corruption and by the time Henry VIII ascended the throne the time was ripe for a change. He appointed royal commissioners to inspect and report on the abbeys and Ramsey was one of the few religious institutions that came out well from these inspections. The commissioner who went to the fens reported that the abbot and his monks were prepared to accept royal sovereignty. He said the monks were "as true and faithful obedientaries to the king's grace as any religious folks in this realm, and (they) live as uprightly as any other, after the best sort of living that hath been among religious folk these many recent years; though more given to ceremonies than was necessary".

The last abbot, who was in charge when this report was submitted, was John de Warboys, or John Lawrence as he is better known. He had been elected either in 1507 or 1508. He evidently anticipated the Dissolution and, as the report indicates, was anxious to cooperate with the king. He was ready to please and to accept the Dissolution, no doubt for the sake of his pension. When it came, it was generous. Abbot John was told he would receive £266.13.6d a year for life with a house at Bodsey and the right to take fuel from woods near Ramsey.

After the Dissolution, Ramsey Abbey, together with several manors, was granted to Richard Williams, later to take the name of Cromwell.

The Cromwells were also given Ramsey Manor and this continued to be handed down in the family until 1674 when the owners, two Cromwell sisters, disposed of it to a Colonel Titus who was MP for Huntingdon in two parliaments after the Restoration. His daughter, Charlotte, left the property to two of her servants. Five or six years later it was sold to Coulson Fellowes. Ramsey Manor is now in the possession of the Fellowes family. In 1887 Edward Fellowes was created Lord de Ramsey.

Of the ancient abbey only the ruins remain. Part of an old gateway, believed to have been the entrance to a building once used as a prison can still be seen. It was probably in fact a porter's lodge with a dungeon underground. A visitor surveying the derelict scene today has to make an imaginative leap to visualise what it would have looked like centuries ago. The imposing abbey would have dominated the little town. It would have been surrounded by trim gardens, orchards and cultivated fields. Inside the walls the corridors would have been alive with the black monks going about their daily business, and in a quiet corridor the abbot would have paced up and down in prayer and meditation with one eye on the look-out for the next opportunity to acquire more land, more wealth and more power.

When St Ivo's shrine had been completed at Ramsey Abbey and his bones had been put on display within it, abbot Eadnoth made sure that news of what he had done was spread around the country. He soon had his reward as pilgrims began passing through Slepe on their way to worship at the shrine. Abbot Eadnoth congratulated himself on his success and then another thought occurred to him. Why not have two shrines, one at Ramsey and one on the spot where the relics had been discovered? The bones of St Ivo's two companions could be sent back to the place where they had been found and then there would be two magnets for pilgrims.

Fig. 4. All that remains of Ramsey Abbey and St Ives Priory: the abbey gateway (*above*), built about 1500; and the walls of the priory barn.

We cannot be certain exactly when St Ivo's priory was completed, but it was before the start of Canute's reign in 1017. It was no Ramsey Abbey. Eadnoth had no intention of building a magnificent building to rival his own, but nevertheless in a small village like Slepe, it stood out and, with the parish church, dominated the landscape.

The bones of St Ivo's companions were duly installed in the shrine and the abbot sent four or five of his monks to run the priory. The black gowned clerics were ruled by a prior also belonging to the abbey. The priory was to remain in Slepe for more than five centuries until the Dissolution. Throughout this period it was never an independent religious house. It was in reality a branch of the abbey. Monks came from and went back to Ramsey on a rota basis.

In 1207 the priory was badly damaged by fire and scars of the blaze were visible for the next 31 years before the building was fully restored. Eventually the building was rededicated in 1238.

As Henry VIII edged closer to the Dissolution of the monasteries, he met with no opposition from John Lawrence, then abbot of Ramsey Abbey. When the king's men demanded the surrender of the abbey, they met only compliance. The abbey passed into regal hands on November 22, 1539. It was a sad, muted surrender for one of the greatest and proudest of England's religious foundations.

When news that the royal emissaries were heading for Ramsey reached St Ives priory, the prior, Robert Huchyn ordered his monks to return to their parent house where they watched the act of submission. The prior remained on alone until, a few days later, it was his turn to surrender a religious house. He was given permission to live in the chapel on the bridge and was also awarded a £12 a year pension.

A few years later, a Thomas Audley took a 21-year lease of the priory property. He and his wife Elizabeth took up residence in the priory. Audley was a member of the Royal Household and made frequent trips to London. He was a staunch supporter of Henry VIII. The house's history becomes difficult to trace at this point, but it is fairly certain that within 20 years of the Dissolution it had been razed to the ground and was a welcome source of stone for masons. Much of the original stonework might have been used for a new house Thomas Audley built, named Priory House.

Priory House changed hands regularly as the years went by and from time to time was extended or rebuilt. Until the last century two relics of the ancient priory were in existence. They were a barn and a dovecote. In 1858 the barn had to be pulled down because it had fallen into such a bad state that it was unsafe.

Herbert Norris in his *History of St Ives*, first published in 1889, confirms that the barn had been a granary in the eighteenth century. In its later years it became a public building and was used intermittently as a theatre. According to Norris when digging was done to erect the new Priory House many human bones were discovered. These were probably the remains of monks. The barn was 92 feet long and 35 feet wide. It had a lofty roof and was supported by two rows of four lofty and massive oak columns.

By 1870 the house had passed to Charles Coote and his wife Agnes. They decided to demolish the building and replace it with a more modern one. It is not known what prompted this decision, but it meant that the house originally built by Thomas Audley along with the alterations made over three centuries, was lost. It was while the new building was being constructed that the human bones came to light. The new Priory House was completed by the end of 1870, as it appears in the national census of 1871.

In 1877 Mrs Coote, now widowed, vacated Priory House which was then rented by Frederic Warren, a future mayor of St Ives. During the last century the house was mainly occupied by Frederic Warren and his heirs. In 1951 ownership passed to St Ives Rural District Council. In 1956 the late Robert Jude, while digging in his garden at Willow Bank, was startled to discover the carved figure of a nude woman. It was a pre-Christian carving in stone, lacking both arms and legs. The upper portion of its head above the eyes had been levelled and looked unattractive, but the body was undeniably that of a woman. In contrast to the indifference to reality with which the rest of the body had been carved, the genitals were accurately reproduced. The carving appeared to have suffered from fire damage and it may have been unearthed while the Priory was being built and placed by the monks on a wall. If so, then it could have been damaged in the fire of 1207. The monks would have had no scruples about exhibiting a plainly pagan figure on holy walls. Superstition was rife, and they would have felt this fertility symbol might have supernatural powers, and that to throw it away might have been tempting providence.

The figure was on display at an exhibition mounted by the Norris Museum in the summer of 1982. When the exhibition closed the carving was returned to Mr Jude. After his death it was never found. In 1974 changes in the structure of local government resulted in the abolition of the St Ives Rural District Council, and the ownership of Priory House passed to Huntingdon District Council. In the summer of 1981 the house was bought and occupied by Stephenson Smart and Company, the local accountants.

Chapter 4
Domesday

By the middle of the eleventh century Slepe was starting to show the first signs of prosperity. It was no longer an obscure river-bank village, the accidental discovery of St Ivo's remains had put it on the pilgrimage map. This in turn led to the residents of Slepe acquiring a certain sophistication. As more and more miracles were reported at St Ivo's shrine, pilgrims began to be attracted not only from all over England, but also from across the English Channel.

The villagers would have watched these newcomers arriving to pray at the shrine and to bathe in the spring. They would have noted their strange languages, their modes of dress and the manner in which they lived. Uneducated serfs would not have been able to communicate with this new breed of pilgrims, but the prior and his monks would have had no difficulty in doing so. Whatever they learnt from their continental visitors would have seeped down to the villagers in the form of gossip. Some of the information might have become distorted in the re-telling, but no one in Slepe could have been left in any doubt that there were lands over the seas, populated by people basically the same as Englishmen despite their different customs, habits and ways of speaking.

After surviving the excitements of the early part of the century, the village relapsed into the routine way of life characteristic of Saxon times. It would have been a fairly relaxed routine. Certainly the villagers were by now living much better lives than those led by their intrepid ancestors who founded Slepe. Several families had acquired land and wealth. The countryside was fertile and crops were good. The village was still surrounded by open fields, but it was steadily growing, and some of the new houses were substantially built. The entire village was under the rule of the abbot of Ramsey Abbey, but by and large this rule was exerted in a benign manner. So long as a villager paid his dues to the prior, obeyed the laws, and did not fall foul of the bailiffs, his life was largely undisturbed. Every now and then on feast days the entire village would get together for a day of celebration and large quantities of the strong, locally brewed ale would be consumed.

The Norman invasion had no immediate impact upon Slepe. By the time William the Conqueror defeated King Harold at the Battle of Hastings, the main problem the villagers faced was what to call their village which was slowly developing into a small town. Both the names Slepe and St Ives were in use and, to confuse matters further, there was a brief period when the two names were linked. The matter was made even more confusing when some people began referring to the village as St Ivo.

There is no record of Norman incursions into this part of the country following William's accession to the throne of England. Armed bands had roamed the country in Saxon times, and if some Norman nobles led raiders in the vicinity of Slepe, its inhabitants would not have felt that things had changed.

But like every other village in the country Slepe could not avoid the Domesday Book. This massive survey of the country was compiled in 1086. The Saxon Chronicle records: "At midwinter, the king was in Gloucester with his council . . . He had deep consultation with them about this land, how it was occupied and by what sort of men. Then he sent his men all over England, into every shire, commissioning them to find out . . . how much each man had who was an occupier of land in England, either in land or in stock, and how much it was worth".

The survey was astonishingly completed in less than a year. It was unique in Europe when it was drawn up and remained so for several centuries. It was extremely thorough. It named and listed the chief landowners and those who held land from them. The rest of the population of the shires was meticulously counted. It was an enormous job which faced William's commissioners. The majority of the population lived in villages whose houses might be huddled together or scattered through fields. The task of counting heads was very difficult.

Villages were grouped into administrative districts called Hundreds, which in turn formed regions within shires or counties, many of which survive to this day with minor boundary changes. All the information was collected at Winchester and copied into a single volume. In places like Slepe the commissioners faced an additional hazard because of a transient population. The pilgrims had to be weeded out from the local residents. Today, with computers at our disposal, the production of a second Domesday Book would not be so formidable a task. Historians still wonder how William's commissioners succeeded in doing their job in less than twelve months.

The land measurement used for the survey was the hide. A hide was the amount of land considered adequate for one free family, or as much land as could be ploughed by one plough in one year. The word is confusing. It is now normally believed to cover about 120 acres, but the size of acres varied in different parts of the country.

There would have been much excitement when the king's commissioner together with his clerk and other assistants forded the Ouse and arrived in the village. On the evening of his arrival the commissioner would have summoned the bailiffs and reeves and explained the purpose of his visit. He would also have consulted with the prior, to discover how much land the priory owned in the area. He would have realised he faced a problem with the pilgrims. King William had been unequivocal in his instructions. The survey must be accurate, he would not tolerate errors. The villagers would no doubt have discussed this new development well into the night, and have used it as an opportunity for some drinking. They would see no harm in what was proposed and anything that broke the dull round of their lives was welcome.

The entry for Slepe in Domesday reads: "In Slepe the abbot of Ramsey has 20 hides of land liable to tax, and land for 24 ploughs. He keeps in his own control land for three ploughs, apart from the hides already mentioned. He now has in his control three ploughs, 39 villagers and 12 smallholders, who have 20 ploughs. There is a priest, a church, 60 acres of pasture, and woods a league long by half a league wide. In Edward the Confessor's reign all this was worth £20, it is now worth £16. Of this land, three of the abbot's men, Evrard, Ingelrann and Pleines, have four hides. They have there three and a half ploughs, and five villagers and six smallholders who have three ploughs, a church and a priest. This is worth 45 shillings. Sheriff Eustace claims one hide".

It appears the commissioner felt either that Slepe had been over valued at £20 or else that it had depreciated since that figure was placed on it. It seems likely that in 1086 Slepe had two churches, one attached to the priory.

William was apparently a suspicious man. He had said he wanted no errors and no sooner had the first lot of commissioners reported their findings than he sent out a second lot to check up on what their predecessors had done. All errors were to be reported to the monarch personally. One hesitates to imagine what must have happened to any commissioners who had been slipshod the first time round. The victor of Hastings would not have treated them kindly.

The Domesday survey had found Slepe to be a reasonably prosperous community with one slightly unusual feature in that it was a centre for pilgrims. No one could quite make up his mind what to call the place, but otherwise there was nothing unusual about it. As the inhabitants gave their names and details of their income and land holdings to the commissioner, they would have been unaware that they were little more than a quarter of a

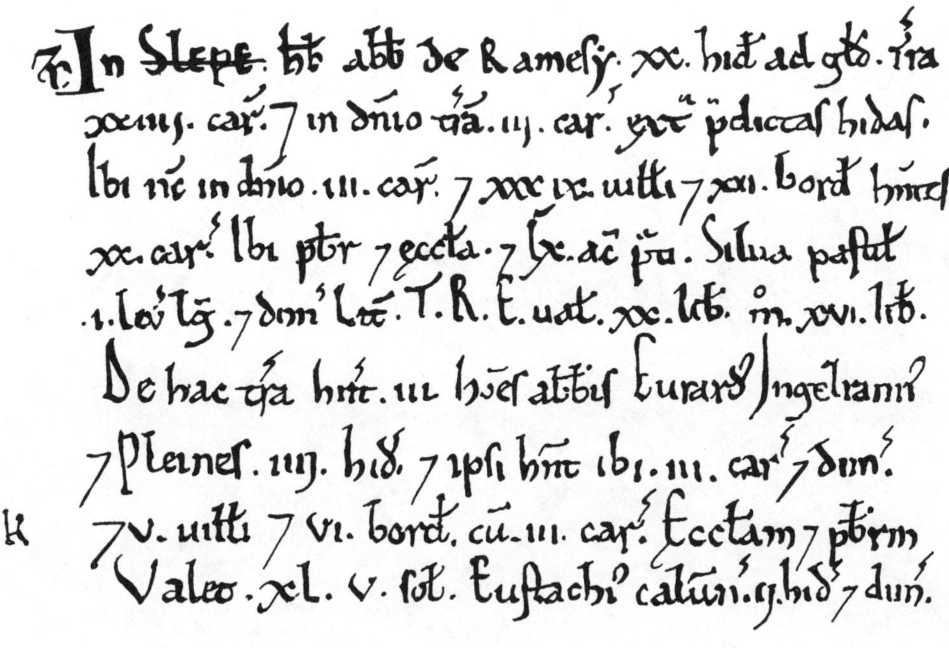

In Slepe ht̄ abb de Ramesy. xx. hid ad gld̄. t̄ra xcuij. car̄. 7 in dn̄io t̄a . iij . car. p̱t̄ p̱dictas hidas. Ibi n̄c in dn̄io . iij . car. 7 xxx ix . uilli 7 xxi . bord h̄ntes xx . car̄. Ibi p̱br 7 eccl̄a . 7 lx . ac p̄ti . Silua pastl̄ . j . leu̱ lg̱ . 7 dim' lat̄. T. R. E. ual. xx . lib. m̄ . xvj . lib. De hac t̄ra h̄nt . iij . h̄oes abb̄is Eurard Ingelrann 7 Plenes . iiij . hid̄ . 7 ipsi h̄nt ibi . iij . car̄ 7 dim. 7 v . uilli 7 vi . bord. cu̱ . iij . car̄. Eccl̄am 7 p̱brm Valeo . xl . v . sol. Eustachi' caluin . ij . hid 7 dim.

Fig. 5.   The entry for Slepe in the Domesday Book.

century away from an event which would bring international renown to their community. In 1110, by which time Slepe was generally regarded as a town, Henry I granted it a charter to hold an annual eight-day Easter Fair. In time this was to lure merchants from all over Europe.

Chapter 5
Princelings and Foreign Merchants

In the Middle Ages the international fairs of England played an important part in the nation's economy, and one of the grandest and most cosmopolitan of these gatherings was the one that took place each Easter in St Ives. It seems strange that St Ives, which had only recently been acknowledged to have become a small town, should host one of these great commercial gatherings, and that royalty as well as wealthy continental traders should have walked the streets of such an insignificant community, but for a brief period each year, St Ives became a teeming city, and enormous sums of money changed hands.

In 1258 the merchants of Douai drew up a list of English fairs which they identified as major markets. They were the fairs at Stamford, Boston, Winchester, Northampton and St Ives. They patronised these fairs and drew in their wake not only royalty, but also noblemen as well as hordes of ordinary citizens and hangers-on including thieves, pickpockets and whores. A special system of justice, known as the piepowder courts, was set up to administer instant justice whenever a fair was held. St Ives was the smallest community to hold an international fair, and to discover the reason why an otherwise anonymous town on the Ouse should become a mercantile magnet, we must study the qualifications that were necessary.

One of the few people to have undertaken intensive research into the medieval fairs of England is Ellen Wedemeyer Moore, who has published two studies on the subject. They were published by the Pontifical Institute of Medieval Studies based in Toronto, Canada, and the author has made a special study of the St Ives fair. One of her studies is entitled "Social Groupings at the Fair of St Ives".

A royal charter was necessary to establish a fair, and during the twelfth and thirteenth centuries, successive English kings exercised their right in this respect liberally. Hundreds of fairs were held across the country but the majority failed to attract any interest outside their local areas. St Ives was one of a handful that did. Nearly all the successful fairs were in the eastern part of England which was an important region for the production of cloth. A site on a river was also important and St Ives, with the Ouse shallow as it flowed past the town, and with an ancient ford available for crossing the river, fulfilled this qualification. Fleets of cargo boats sailed the waters around Europe, and St Ives, which was also conveniently close to the one major road running north to south, opened up a large part of England to these maritime traders.

St Ives fair was created by a charter granted by Henry I in 1110. At about the same time, the abbot of Ramsey Abbey, who owned the town, saw the commercial possibilities and had a crude wooden bridge built across the river. When this bridge was built is not known, but it appears to have been in the beginning of the twelfth century. This would be logical. At the time the abbey was actively promoting the cult of St Ivo. Now the abbey was also in charge of a successful fair. The prelate who ruled the abbey at the time would have been a shrewd businessman, and would have realised that the fair might expand even more if access across the Ouse were made easier. He probably had no idea just how immense this expansion was going to be.

The charter establishing the fair makes one of the last references to the town of Slepe. The king says he gives his permission for a fair to be held "to St Benedict of Ramsey and St Ivo of Slepe". The fair was to be held at Easter and not on St Ivo's feast day which was on April

24. At first it was only a small, local gathering, but interest developed and by the middle of the twelfth century merchants began coming not only from nearby towns, but from as far away as Lincoln, York, Beverley, Leicester, Coventry and Hereford.

In time news of the success of the fair crossed the channel and traders started arriving from Ypres, Ghent, Brabant, Amiens and later from Italy. From time to time some of these visitors settled in the town, a notable example being in about 1338 when a group of Brabant weavers decided to make St Ives their home.

The main trade was in hides, cloth and wool, though other products such as spices, wax and food were also prominent. The cloth trade received a considerable boost when Henry III began sending the royal tailor and other members of his staff to St Ives every Easter. Cloth was the most important commodity at the fairs and the kings of England were the patrons to attract. They had to provide cloth for the gallants of their courts and for the uniforms for their retainers. The queens' needs for lavish gowns for themselves and for their ladies in waiting were extravagant. It was an age when royalty dressed the part and when courtiers robed themselves sumptuously. The men wore elaborate tunics, mantles, hoods and hose, while the women favoured flowing gowns, fur-lined mantles, girdles and wimples. In addition the kings had to furnish all the royal residences with drapes and tapestries.

The royal charter setting up the fair extended the king's peace "to all coming thither, remaining there and returning thence". The charter was signed and dated from Brampton. As the abbots of Ramsey Abbey owned St Ives, they controlled the fair, and St Ives flitted briefly into the papal ken when Pope Innocent II included it in a list of the possessions of the monastery. Succeeding kings regularly confirmed the charter and when King John did so in 1200, the abbot at the time also bought from him the grant of a weekly Monday market.

There followed a series of acrimonious and highly complicated disputes between Henry III and the abbot lasting over several years as to precisely how far the abbey's jurisdiction over the fair extended. The king, who bought very large quantities of cloth at the fair, appointed two wardens to attend it in 1250. Two years later the abbot had the temerity to sue them as well as the royal tailor and another member of the royal household for exceeding their duties. He alleged they were prolonging the fair by up to three weeks, and charging the abbey £15 in rent for houses, stalls and booths.

The case threatened to get out of hand, with the burgesses of Huntingdon, who claimed their bailiffs should collect tolls from travellers coming over the bridge, also becoming involved. The wardens countered by saying they were entitled to charge rents for the period by which they extended the fair. They argued they were entitled to these rents as the booths and stalls were on the king's highway. They also maintained the water on which boats were moored during the fair and from which goods were sold, was owned by the king for two leagues below Huntingdon. These two fine legal points were tossed into the dispute and tempers on both sides became frayed. Reading accounts of this legal wangle today, it all sounds petty. At one stage the incident threatened to disintegrate into comic opera when the king appointed a commission, and two dozen knights rode into the town to consider the matter. The decision of this body is not known as it apparently failed to reach one. This would not be surprising considering the invidious position in which the knights found themselves. To have come out against the king would have inevitably incurred royal displeasure. On the other hand to have decided against Ramsey Abbey would have meant offending an abbot who was locally very powerful.

The affair was eventually solved with the traditional British tendency to compromise, and in 1258 for a fee of 500 marks, and the promise of £50 a year, the king abandoned to the abbot "all profits from the fair however long it might last". The monetary settlement appears to have been based on the Crown's revenue from the fair for the previous year.

Furs, spices, wool, foodstuffs and horses were all traded at the fair, but by far the most important commodity was cloth. This was the product that attracted the continental buyers.

In turn continental cloth was sought after by English merchants, particularly that from Flanders, Douai and Ypres. Italian and French cloth was also marketed but to a lesser extent. The kings of England were extensive buyers. According to the Victoria History of the Counties of England, King Henry III in 1237 purchased 1,100 ells of green and murray, or mulberry coloured cloth for his knights, 180 ells of murray for the royal clerks, 340 ells of murray and green for the serjeants of the court, 40 coarse borel gowns for his grooms, 160 ells of murray and green for ladies' dresses, 80 ells of scarlet cloth and 18 hoods besides "finer stuffs, furs and wax". As an ell in today's terms equalled about 45 inches, it is clear that royal buyers gave a boost to trade.

Wool was another important product at these fairs which were open to all. Anyone, no matter how humble, could trade at them. While the international wholesalers tended to do business in certain specific areas and set out magnificent stalls displaying the most expensive goods, there was nothing to stop the ordinary street hawker setting up a stall if he could find a spot on which to mark it out.

All this commercial activity tended to draw tricksters and quick-witted salesmen to fairs. The Court Rolls illustrate this. We read that John, son of John of Eltisley, complained of Roger the barber that he was in Ramsey in January 1288 when he met Roger who claimed he could cure John of baldness. John paid him ninepence and the following day Roger swathed John's head in plaster and repeated the treatment the following day. He then left Ramsey and, more importantly from John's point of view, he left his patient as bald as ever.

The two men had apparently run into each other at St Ives fair and John hauled Roger before the court. After a crisp exchange in court, Roger walked out without permission. He was arrested and brought back next day and ordered to repay the ninepence and pay sixpence in damages.

Roger was evidently one of the numerous quacks who were constantly roving the countryside. They always attended fairs and markets where they could be confident of finding enough gullible people to part with their money.

Jean Jusserand writing at the turn of this century on English Wayfaring Life in the Middle Ages, gives examples of the sort of patter which must day after day have been heard in Bridge Street and on Market Hill . . . "My good friends, I am not one of those poor preachers, nor one of those herbalists who stand in front of the churches with their miserable, ill-sewn cloaks, who carry bags and boxes, and spread out a carpet. But I belong to a lady who is named madam Trote of Salerno who makes a kerchief of her ears, and whose eyebrows hang down as silver chains behind her shoulders: know that she is the wisest in all the far quarters of the globe. My lady sends us into many lands . . . into the forests of Ardennes to kill wild beasts in order to extract good ointment from them".

This would go on until the salesman had drawn a crowd. He would then unveil his "guaranteed" cure and, having made some quick sales, would normally vanish from the town and move on elsewhere.

Over-confident salesmen like Roger ran a hazardous existence. If they hung around too long they would, sooner or later, meet someone whom they had tricked and would find themselves before the court.

The fairs had a curious system of debt collection. Debts contracted at one fair could be claimed back at the next one on the circuit. A certain Thomas Peyt who had agreed at Boston in 1293 to sell eleven sacks of wool to two partners to be paid for at the next fair in Northampton, sued for and obtained his money at St Ives. When a Bluntisham trader went to London in November 1292 for cloth, he promised to pay at Stamford. He defaulted, but the London draper caught up with him at St Ives and had him arrested. A Bordeaux wine merchant who sold wine to some Norwich men at Boston in 1273 searched in vain for them throughout 1274, but came across them at St Ives in 1275 and brought them to justice.

While traders liked the prestige that a royal patron could bestow, many of them dreaded the arrival of the royal tailor. This was because English kings were notoriously bad payers. With frequent foreign wars and incessant feuding with nobles, the kings had constantly to spend large amounts of money on arms, and this was a drain on the exchequer. If they bought from a small trader the poor man stood a good chance of going bankrupt. Some merchants regarded the advent of royal buyers with open dismay. In 1261 Henry III was reported to be eleven years in debt for cloth he bought at various fairs. In fact some of these debts were never paid.

Merchants were normally grouped together in various parts of the fair. Cattle dealers, butchers and tanners together with the sellers of fresh produce would be separated from the drapers, woolmongers and sellers of spices. Efforts were also made to ensure goods were not sold just outside the town and later resold at the fair at inflated prices. There were also rules of standard weights and measures. At St Ives the bailiffs were responsible for placing the Ramsey Abbey seal on standard bottles of ale and wine and for rejecting sub-standard ones. There were also rules for the standard weight of bales of cloth and fines for infringing these rules were substantial. One group of continental merchants was fined £1,000 at St Ives in 1269.

The site of the fair was of great importance. It had to meet three requirements. It should make trade easy in a wide range of goods, it should provide for the health and safety of fairgoers and it should bring in profits for its owners. This last qualification was simple to fulfil in the case of St Ives which was owned by the abbots of Ramsey Abbey. The abbots merely gave over the town to the organisers of the fair. They leased out the buildings whose normal tenants had no alternative but to give up the use of their front rooms and to retire with their families to the back of the house, sometimes into just one room for the duration of the fair. For a brief period the abbots were, in effect, receiving double rents, and rents during fair time were high. Tenants who leased houses from the abbey for normal housing reasons always had to agree to a contract which stated they had tenancy rights ". . . saving for the lord abbot the possession of the front during fair times".

For additional sales facilities the abbots had wooden stalls built each year, the men who built them being manorial tenants who thus discharged part of the annual service they had to provide free for the abbot. The market area followed the established street pattern of the town. It began in Bridge Street and, as it advanced, turned left and right towards the parish church and Market Hill respectively. Permanent buildings flanked these streets and stalls and booths were erected in front of them. Sales were also made from barges moored in the river along the Quay. The abbots took rents from all these temporary shops.

No one could take rents or conduct business in any way that harmed the abbey's interests. Trading in the rear of houses was a crime. William of Yelling was charged with contempt and trespass for renting a room to two merchants and for allowing goods to change hands "outside the body of the fair", that is to say in a back room. The final limits of the fair were the tollbooth on the bridge, and the gates on the road leading into the town from the north.

In the interests of safety a careful eye was kept on stalls selling cooked meat. This was necessary because in a packed area where the majority of the buildings were made of wood and where vast amounts of cloth were standing out in the open, the risk of fire breaking out from over-fanned flames was high. At one fair the jurors of Bridge Street complained that "four cooks in Bridge Street have their little sheds made of reeds much too near the cookfire to the great danger of the town". All householders within the fair site had to make sure they had a ditch filled with water ready for use in an emergency. Fines for disobeying this injunction are regularly recorded in the fair court rolls. Great damage was suffered in some fair fires, but St Ives appears to have been fortunate or particularly careful. The town seems to have had only one fire and that one was not too severe.

Prostitutes and lepers were barred from fairs but this did not stop them from getting in.

Fig. 6. Traces of St Ives fair: the Quay (*above*), where merchants unloaded their wares; and the Market Hill, where part of the fair was held.

For the prostitutes in particular, a fair was an excellent arena in which to operate. One noted harlot who made her living by travelling from fair to fair was Dulcie of Oxford. The delectable Dulcie hawked her charms around the country and was a regular attender at St Ives where she made frequent appearances before the piepowder courts.

The fair court rolls tell us that Ralph Keyes was fined sixpence for sheltering lepers in his house "to the great danger of the neighbours". Nicholas Turgy was fined a shilling because he was reported to "receive certain prostitutes". Another entry reads: "It is presented by the jurors of Bridge Street that Avenand receives prostitutes, therefore he is fined, but his fine is condoned because he is a receiver of alms". In other words, it was all right to sleep with prostitutes if you were so poor that you could not pay a fine.

To maintain law and order the abbots of the abbey organised a system under which constables and watchmen were responsible for maintaining peace, and every householder was responsible for the security of his property. The constables were responsible to the bailiffs. There were two separate judicial areas, Bridge Street and The Green. These two areas each elected their own jurors who brought complaints before the court.

The court rolls record a typical case. "Isabella Nutrix of Cambridge complains of Hugo Tapping of Boston and says the same Hugo on the Sunday before the feast of St Dunstan in the 19th year of the reign of King Edward, badly injured her next to her right eye with a piece of wood while she was sitting and drinking in the house of John of Quy in the town of St Ives, to her damage forty shillings". Hugo claims it was an accident and that he never meant the woman any harm. It was horseplay that got out of hand. As he admits he hit Isabella, he is fined, but his fine is suspended because he is poor.

Although the fair began to decline towards the end of the thirteenth century, the abbot was still receiving more than £120 from stallages alone in the 1280s, and until 1332 the abbey paid without protest its annual £50 to the Crown. By 1324 royal purchases were confined to the fairs at St Ives and Boston, but were still extensive. The 1290s were a particularly lean time from which the international fairs never really recovered. Foreign wars contributed in some part to this decline. A series of wars led the Crown to levy heavy taxes during this period, many of them on wool, causing disruption in the cloth trade. The appeal of fairs for drapers and wool merchants was thereby diminished.

Ellen Wedemeyer Moore believes the increasing dominance of London in commerce also contributed. By 1300 the capital controlled much of the English trade in wool, cloth, furs, fish and grain. Edward I established the Royal Wardrobe in London and so it was no longer necessary for his buyers to travel the country looking for expensive materials at fairs. While international fairs throughout the country grew less and less important, the fairs themselves continued to play an important role in the life of rural England.

Historians differ about the population of St Ives in the thirteenth century, but it was probably about 800. For a brief period the original settlement of Slepe was called The Green during this century. It was merged into St Ives as the two communities, separated then by what is now The Waits, expanded and grew towards each other.

The Black Death may have been another reason why fairs began to lose their appeal and historian Andrew Woodger advanced his own theory in his book *Ancient Huntingdonshire* which was published in 1986. He suggested that the slow decline which started at the end of the thirteenth century developed into a landslide because of new technology. One of the main commodities traded at the fair was *borel* or *burel*, used to make the tunics widely worn in medieval England.

Woodger says that in the middle of the thirteenth century, while English weavers were still producing cloth on primitive looms, their counterparts in Flanders discovered a far more efficient machine capable of weaving faster and turning out better cloth. The Flemish weavers guarded their secret for several years, and by the time news of the invention crossed the Channel, it was too late. Flanders had virtually taken control of the international cloth trade.

England was reduced to the humiliating position of exporting to Flanders, and later to Italy, English wool which was woven abroad and then reimported as cloth.

The one remaining relic of the days when weavers came from Europe to carry on their trade in St Ives is the street named Tenterleas. Lea meant a meadow and tenter was the name for the rectangular wooden frame with tenterhooks attached on which wool was dried and stretched after dyeing. The name evokes visions of Brabant weavers bent over their looms, busily plying their craft.

International fairs threw up a new form of justice known as the piepowder court. It was a humble court confined to markets or fairs to adjudicate and pronounce on disputes between itinerant merchants. The distinguished jurist Sir William Blackstone described it as "the lowest and sometimes the most expeditious court of justice known to the law of England".

Some legal historians believe the term "piepowder", from the French *pieds poudrés*, "dusty feet", arose because justice was dispensed as speedily as the dust could fall or be removed from the feet of litigants. Others claim it was because the courts were filled with people with dusty feet who had wandered from fair to fair. Modern textbooks dismiss them in a few vague paragraphs while earlier writers tend to differ in their explanations of their functions. One of the fullest printed sources for them is contained in the court rolls of the St Ives fair from 1270 to 1324, considered by some experts to be unrivalled. A copy of the rolls can be seen in the Norris Library.

According to Ellen Wedemeyer Moore piepowder courts were themselves a source of livelihood and an economic attraction of the fairs. Professional administrators, generally one steward and six to eight bailiffs, were employed to organise the courts. The steward would preside over his court and make procedural decisions in the name of the abbot. These would include decisions about how a defendant should plead, decisions about the fines to be imposed and decisions about suspending fines when the defendant was too old or too sick to be penalised.

The bailiffs were also specialists. They were responsible for the rapid dispensation of justice at the court. Each took charge of a certain number of cases each year and had to know what was going on from day to day. In St Ives the abbot was responsible for the administration of justice and he appointed the steward and the bailiffs. The two separately recognised areas of the town, Bridge Street and The Green, appointed jurors who brought complaints before the court.

The most striking feature of these courts was their summary procedure. In the twelfth century in some parts of the country custom dictated that pleas concerning wandering merchants should be settled "before the third tide". Speed was of the essence since merchants were transient visitors to the town and might stay only a day or two. This is made clear by studying a case held before the King's Bench in the reign of Edward IV. The judges laid down that if a defendant failed to appear immediately when summoned, his goods were to be seized forthwith, valued and sold.

For the period between 1270 and 1324 St Ives has an almost full series of rolls and they show that about four and a half thousand names appear at least once. This shows how busy the courts were and how they formed an essential part of the fairs. Practically every type of offence could be judged before a piepowder court, whether it involved trading, illegal hawking, assault, theft, the breaking of a contract, drunkenness or prostitution.

We read in the rolls that: "Emma Hauteyn complains of Richard Burdun because, whereas she rented a house from him during the fair for 21 pence, on the condition that he, Richard, would receive no prostitutes in his row, Richard has not kept the agreement and has in fact received prostitutes". This was in 1295. Three years later the rolls record: "Willelmus Verun complains of Rogerus Lomb and says that whereas he, William, rented a certain house in the town of St Ives from a certain Robertus Belaunt de Wystowe to keep sixteen hams which he had for sale, the said Roger came there on Monday after Ascension Day and took and detained from him the said hams, each worth sixteen pence, causing him damage of one half mark. The said Roger is present and denies etc. and says that he did not take away any of the said hams except two, and he took those two because Robertus Belaunt owed him, Roger, two shillings in silver for a certain house which Robert had rented from him. Afterwards the parties came to agreement . . ."

In the time of Edward I the courts sat daily except on Sundays, but in later years they met less frequently. A plea lodged at one session would normally be heard the following day. Professional pleaders or attorneys were often hired by litigants. Charles Gross, in his *Select Cases Concerning the Law Merchant*, published in 1908, talks of the constant annoyance caused to the authorities by "the great influx of harlots", who were often "harboured by barbers". The reason for this is not hard to guess. Most barber's shops in the Middle Ages had bathing rooms at the rear of their premises, and these places, where men would strip before entering the water, would be obvious targets for enterprising whores.

The courts were very busy, bustling places, hearing cases ranging from petty personal squabbles to important commercial suits. Many of the cases related to the recovery of unpaid rents, or to debts contracted by merchants. Only cases concerning loss of limb or life were referred to royal judges. The speed with which justice was dispensed is evident from some of the entries in the fair court rolls. At the 1270 fair Arnulph Scutebunt was charged with selling goods from the rear rooms of houses. His plea is not recorded, but whatever it was, he was instantly fined two shillings and told he must pay the lord abbot a shilling for a licence to sell outside the fair area. Denis of Cambridge, a clerk, came before the court and acknowledged he owed John of Hamerton two marks of silver. He swore he would repay this debt whereupon John demanded guarantors. Denis was unable to provide these and so an order was made to arrest Denis "as often as he may be found".

Another case involves William Redknave, whose neighbours complained he sheltered not a single prostitute, but several of them. No fine is recorded against Redknave's name, but there is the succint comment: "he is poor". Two days later another man escaped without penalty on an identical charge. It appears the steward was getting irritated at this stream of defendants who could not keep away from harlots because the next item reads: "It is ordered that Ralph of Armston and all his fellow bailiffs shall cause the bodies of all the said harlots, wherever they may be found within the bounds and lists of the fair, to be arrested and brought to the court and held in safe custody".

Banishment from the fair was a frequent punishment in addition to a fine for prostitutes who came before the court. Dulcie of Oxford's visits to St Ives often ended with her walking wearily over the bridge to head for either Huntingdon or Cambridge. On one occasion after being fined the almost statutory sixpence, she escaped a rider of banishment only because William Manger and Hugh of Swinford pledged before the Court that she would behave decently. The rolls do not record whether William and Hugh were married and, if they were, what their wives thought of their chivalrous action.

A couple from Pontefract convicted of stealing a pair of shoes worth twopence-halfpenny, were ordered to leave the town and "never more hereafter return thereto". Some of the cases concerning debts involving wealthy traders were very complicated, with charges and counter charges being brought by litigants on both sides.

Violence, probably caused by excessive indulgence in alcohol was never very far beneath the surface. Four Broughton men who had been assigned to keep watch at the foot of the bridge against intruders during the night, fell asleep, and some of the booths and stalls were ransacked "by evildoers". All four appointed guardians were fined a shilling. A jury of merchants and citizens found that William of Tilney assaulted John Sherman "with vile words, calling him knave and thief". William was fined a shilling and ordered to pay two shillings damages.

A more vicious assault involved Walter of Longbargh who complained that Henry of Bythorn had two days earlier, in front of the booths of the Brabant weavers, maliciously assaulted him and thrown him down a well. Having survived this ordeal, Walter came to court and a long argument ensued, with Henry vigorously denying the charge. In the end the matter was settled by a compromise reached out of court.

Even after the fair went into decline, the formalities continued for many years. Year after year officials rode over from Ramsey Abbey to declare the opening of an event that had long since lost its glamour. Each year more and more "fronts" were not let because of the lack of traders and the piepowder courts ceased functioning. The opening ceremony continued to be held until 1473, by which date the fair appears to have expired. We know that by 1511 it was officially abandoned. The great St Ives fair, which had been born to the accompaniment of a majestic royal charter, died slowly upon a sigh.

Chapter 6
The Farmer of St Ives

Oliver Cromwell's connections with Huntingdonshire, including a five-year spell during which he lived and farmed at St Ives, are well documented. What is difficult to judge now is just what sort of early life he lived, particularly during his youth at Huntingdon and later as a student at Cambridge. Loved and hated in equal measure during his lifetime, his death resulted in the growth of a Cromwell legend. Some historians rushed to worship at his shrine. Others, many of them highly unreliable, sought to prove that he was little short of a devil incarnate.

The future Lord Protector was born at Huntingdon on April 25, 1599. He was christened four days later in St John's Church, and the entry in the church registers still exists: "In the year of our Lord 1599, Oliver, the son of Robert Cromwell, gentleman, and of Elizabeth his wife, born on the 25th day of April and baptised on the 29th of the same month". Against this entry some anti-commonwealth visitor has inscribed a message which appears to read: "England's plague for five years". The book containing the entry is now kept under strict security at the County Record Office in Huntingdon.

Little survives from Cromwell's childhood apart from a few isolated facts, some legend and a good deal of questionable gossip. He is reported to have wrestled in play as a child with the future Charles I, and to have had much the better of these youthful exchanges as he was more sturdily built than the future monarch. His headmaster at his Huntingdon school was Dr Thomas Beard, a stern anti-papist who taught his pupils to fear God's wrath as the Almighty never forgave his transgressors. It may well be that Dr Beard made a lasting impression on one particular pupil and laid the foundation for Cromwell's puritanical zeal.

Legend is not hard to come by when researching Cromwell's life as a young man. According to his detractors he spent a dissolute youth drinking and gaming in Huntingdon's public houses. According to his more vehement critics his reputation was so bad that publicans closed their doors when they saw him approaching. They feared the brawling he indulged in after a few drinks, and were also fed up with chasing him for money he constantly owed them. These stories are impossible to substantiate as is the legend concerning the monkey. It is said that while a baby at Hinchingbrooke, he was seized from his cot by a monkey who ran with the infant up on to a rooftop. Cromwell's life is said to have been saved only after a frantic, almost farcical chase.

What is known is that Cromwell went from Huntingdon to Cambridge. His master at Sidney Sussex College was Dr Samuel Ward, a man of strong Puritan views. Dr Ward would have built on the foundation already laid by Dr Beard. These two men were responsible for the stern, unbending attitude towards divine worship that was so marked a trait of Cromwell's later life. Years later, when the victorious parliamentary leaders were meeting to discuss the king's fate, Cromwell is said to have spent hours on end "wrestling with his conscience", as he himself put it, to see whether God would give him a sign that the monarch's life should be spared.

Another breed of historians, however, insist that Cromwell's time in Cambridge was simply an extension of his debauched life in Huntingdon. They claim he whiled away his time at the university drinking, womanising and neglecting his studies. These stories have been given some credence by Cromwell's own enigmatic recollection of his youth. As a mature man

Fig. 7. The frontispiece of a hostile biography of Cromwell published in 1665: the Protector is shown with a noose round his neck, a symbol of divine justice.

he once remarked: "I lived in and loved darkness and hated the light. I was a chief, the chief of sinners". That clipped observation has been used to prove that the man who was later to "wrestle with his conscience", had spent a dissolute and anything but puritanical youth.

Hard evidence of youthful misconduct has not survived, and it is likely that Oliver Cromwell behaved no better and no worse than most of his fellow students. His intellectual talents were limited, and he enjoyed country sports. He probably spent more time in hunting, fishing and playing games than he spent in the lecture room or in his study with his books. That would not set him apart from the majority of Cambridge students.

The origins of the Cromwell family are somewhat obscure. One of the most distinguished historians to have researched Oliver Cromwell's life was the Rev. Mark Noble, whose *Memoirs of Cromwell* was published in 1784. According to Noble, a genealogical tree was drawn up in 1602 by Sir Henry Cromwell, the grandfather of the Protector. It included the ancient Welsh family of the Lords of Powys from whom Sir Henry was descended on the male side. The family bore the name Williams, before changing it to Cromwell. Noble states that the genealogy demands little attention "as it goes back to barbaric ages and a still more savage country", until we come to Morgan Williams.

He was a gentleman of Glamorgan, said to be in favour with Henry VII, and may have been a privy councillor. Sir Richard Williams was his eldest son and heir. Details of Richard's early life are not known, but he was brought to the court of Henry VIII by Thomas Cromwell, one of the king's favourites, who was to become Earl of Essex and a Knight of the Garter. Morgan Williams, according to the pedigree, married a sister of Thomas Cromwell. This is disputed, but it is certain that Richard was Thomas's nephew, and that Thomas married a widow of a Williams.

Richard's powerful introduction to court, as well as his qualities, soon brought him to the notice of the king. Following a Roman Catholic uprising in Lincolnshire which became known as the Pilgrimage of Grace, Henry sent a group of hand-picked men to visit monasteries and other religious houses. Sir Richard was one of these, and the king was so pleased with his work, he became a royal favourite. In 1538 he was granted the nunnery of Hinchingbrooke in Huntingdonshire. He was later given possession of Grey-Friars Abbey, Great Yarmouth and of Ramsey Abbey.

It is believed that Henry suggested to Sir Richard that he adopt the name of Cromwell, as the name Williams had little standing in England. He may also have made the change in honour of his uncle. When Essex was executed in 1540 – the life of a royal favourite could be a hazardous one – Sir Richard contrived to continue in favour and a year later was appointed High Sheriff of Huntingdonshire and Cambridge.

He also became an MP for the county in the parliament which began in January 1542. He went to France as General of Infantry when war broke out the following year, all officers of the force being carefully chosen and "all right hardie and valiant knights, esquires and gentlemen". In 1544 Sir Richard was appointed Constable of Berkeley Castle in Gloucestershire.

Sir Richard made a will in 1545 leaving his estates in Huntingdonshire, Cambridgeshire and Bedfordshire to his eldest son, Henry, a common name for eldest sons in the Cromwell family. Sir Richard had married in 1518 Frances, the daughter of Sir Thomas Murfyn, Lord Mayor of London. She had died in 1533, having borne two sons, Henry and Francis. Sir Henry, as he was to become, was highly esteemed by Queen Elizabeth and she visited him at Hinchingbrooke in August 1564 on her way back to London after a visit to Cambridge University.

Sir Henry was elected an MP in 1563 and was four times High Sheriff. He was also one of a group of commissioners appointed to look into the problem of fen drainage. He lived at Ramsey in the summer, and at Hinchingbrooke during the winter. He was known for his generosity, and is said, when he visited Ramsey, to have thrown money on the streets as he passed by. He married twice, and his second wife's death was directly responsible for the trial and execution of the witches of Warboys.

This trial of a simple fenland family of three was one of the more spectacular witchcraft trials of the 16th century. It was an age of superstition when simple people could easily be persuaded that any event slightly out of the ordinary was due to supernatural causes. People went in dread of witchcraft, and anyone accused of dabbling in the occult was in mortal danger from the moment the allegation was made.

The Samuel family lived in a thatched cottage which once stood on the site of the Clock Tower garage in Warboys. The mother, Alice, worked as a sort of district nurse, tending the sick and elderly. Robert Throgmorton was one of Warboys' most influential residents and lived at the manor house with his wife and five daughters. In 1588 he led a contingent of soldiers sent to the east coast to guard against any landing of Spanish forces. When he returned home a year later he found that his daughters were ill and that the eldest, Joan, was being nursed by Alice. Despite being treated by a doctor, Joan became worse, apparently suffering fits, during which she would point to Alice and accuse her of being a witch. Another doctor was called from Cambridge, and he came to the conclusion that the girl's fits were due to "diabolical agencies".

Despite this disturbing diagnosis, the Throgmorton family took no action and continued to employ Alice. The village, however, was by now alive with rumour. Villagers pointed out that not only did Alice wear a mob cap, but that she had a pet chicken which followed her everywhere. It was believed that the chicken was Alice's "familiar", the means by which she communicated with the devil. The Samuel family might have survived this gossip had not Lady Cromwell arrived on a visit to the Throgmortons.

She openly accused Alice of witchcraft and one afternoon snatched off the old woman's cap, cut off a lock of hair and told Mrs Throgmorton to burn it in the fire. As Alice left the room she was alleged to have looked at Lady Cromwell and muttered: "I've never harmed you, as yet". That night Lady Cromwell fell ill and suffered nightmares about Alice Samuel and the pet chicken. It was the start of a long illness from which she never recovered. She died in 1592.

Meanwhile efforts were made to extract a confession from Alice Samuel, and she was eventually brought before the Bishop of Lincoln at Buckden. He committed her to the Huntingdon Assizes, and when she arrived at the town's jail she found her husband and daughter already there. While the trial of the three was going on, her Huntingdon jailer died suddenly and his daughter began to suffer fits similar to those of Joan Throgmorton. All three Samuels were found guilty of witchcraft in 1593 and were hanged in the market place. According to custom their naked bodies were put on display so that people could examine them for marks such as warts and moles, considered to be the marks of the devil.

Noble, referring to the trial and execution writes: "As this lady (Lady Cromwell) died of a lingering illness, popular rumour at the time attributed her death to witchcraft . . . at that time an accusation of the most serious consequence, and a poor, inoffensive family fell victim to the folly and cruelty of the age. John Samuel, his wife Alice and their daughter Ann, were ridiculously supposed to be the authors of the lady's death and were committed to prison. The mother, who seems by age to have been weak and decrepit, was so seized and tortured in prison, that her faculties, much impaired before, became now entirely lost, and at length she confessed any, the most strange fooleries, that the malice and folly of her enemies could devise. In consequence of which they were all, in defiance of commonsense, tried before Mr Justice Fenner on April 4, 1593 and convicted of the fact of not only being the cause of the death of Lady Cromwell, but also of bewitching five of Mr Throgmorton's children and seven of his servants, the gaoler's man etc.

"No mercy, we may imagine, would be shown to these unbefriended victims when even majesty degraded itself by writing the most idle nonsense (some years later) to prove, not only

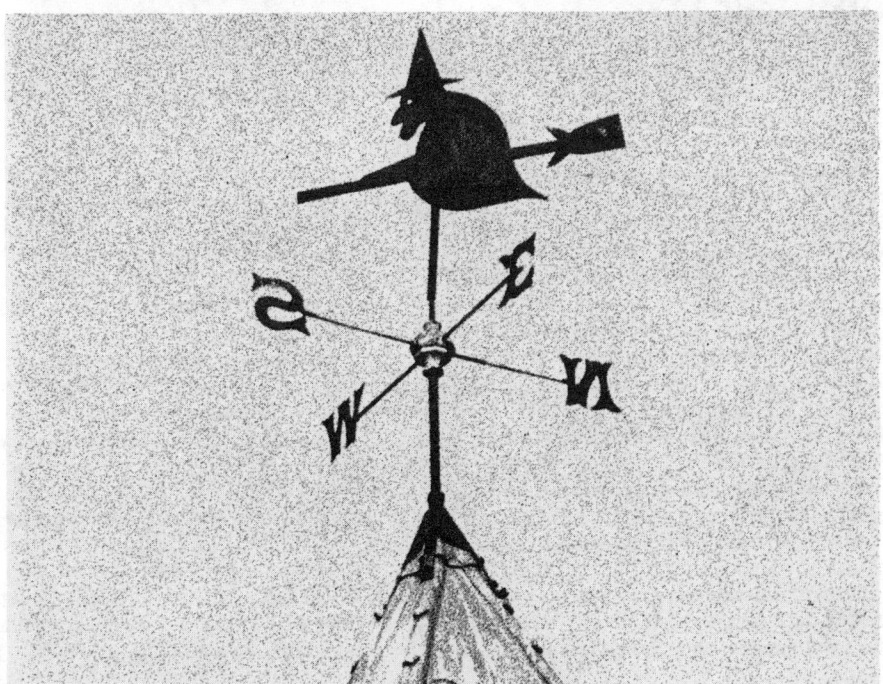

Fig. 8. Oliver Cromwell's death mask (*above*), in the Norris Museum; and a witch of Warboys, as shown on the weather-vane of the village clock tower.

that there were witches, but recommending certain means to be used as infallible ways to discover them". The goods of the Samuel family were found to be worth £40. These were forfeited to Sir Henry who was lord of all the land around Ramsey including Warboys. The widower declined to accept this offering from the grave and gave the money to the local corporation on condition it was used to get a preacher once a year from Queens' College, Cambridge, to preach a sermon declaiming against witchcraft in a Huntingdon church. This sermon continued to be preached until 1812.

Sir Henry had several children by his first wife, but none by his ill-fated second. His eldest child was Oliver who was to be knighted and who inherited the bulk of the family fortune. His second son, Robert, was the father of the Protector. Sir Oliver was very popular in Huntingdon for which he was MP for many years. He was knighted by Queen Elizabeth in 1598 while he was High Sheriff. He frequently entertained James I at Hinchingbrooke, and probably also entertained Charles I before his accession to the throne.

On his first visit James was impressed with the lavishness of his host's hospitality. As the king was preparing to leave Hinchingbrooke, he was presented with valuable gifts including: "a large, elegantly wrought standing cup of gold, goodly horses, deep mouthed hounds and divers hawks of excellent wing".

Sir Oliver was also in favour with Charles I. He lived beyond his means by trying to impress royalty and had to sell much of his estates to meet debts. He sold Hinchingbrooke to Sir Sydney Montagu and went to live in Ramsey. Sir Oliver was an active royalist during the Civil War and continued to spend money in the royalist cause. At great cost he raised forces on the king's behalf and also gave quantities of cash to the royal army. He made sure his sons fought with the cavaliers and made himself highly unpopular among the Roundheads.

His nephew and godchild Oliver, later the Protector, called on his uncle at Ramsey at the head of a strong body of horse. While the nephew displayed filial courtesy by refusing to wear his hat in his uncle's presence and even asked for his blessing, he did not leave until he had disarmed his uncle and stripped him of his silver plate. On a second visit Oliver demanded a large sum of money from his uncle who replied that he was unable to raise so large a sum. Oliver, now a lieutenant general with the parliamentary forces, threatened to sack Ramsey unless he received payment. This threat frightened the old man, who agreed to meet his nephew on the town's bridge.

Oliver was accompanied to the meeting by a body of horsemen and a compromise was reached whereby Sir Oliver supplied his nephew with 40 saddle horses and £1,000 in cash. It was the last meeting between uncle and nephew. Sir Oliver died at the age of 92 and was buried at dead of night – to prevent, according to popular rumour, his body being snatched by creditors. Because of his extravagant lifestyle and expensive espousal of the royalist causes, he died heavily in debt despite having sold many of his lands during his lifetime.

John Cromwell, Sir Oliver's third son, fought with the royalists. According to one report he once went to see his cousin, then a lieutenant general, armed with pleas from several European princes for the Roundheads to spare the king's life. The meeting is said to have taken place in London and the future Protector is reported to have said it was not up to him to take the decision, adding: "I have prayed and fasted for the king, but no return that way has yet been made to me".

At this John Cromwell is supposed to have slammed shut the door of the room, leading the parliamentary commander to believe he was about to be assassinated. But John merely took out the written petitions he was carrying with the words: "cousin, this is no time to trifle with words; see here, it is now in your power not only to make yourself, but your family, relatives and posterity, happy and honourable forever. Otherwise, as they have changed their name before from Williams to Cromwell, so now they must be forced to change it again, for the fact will bring such an ignominy upon the whole generation of them as no time will be able to efface".

Oliver asked John to return to his lodgings and await news. At 1-am John received a message that the council of officers had been "seeking God" and that Oliver himself was doing the same thing and that "it had been resolved by all the king must die".

These momentous events were a long way in the future when Cromwell was passing his time at Cambridge indulging in field sports and keeping only a cursory eye on his curriculum. His studies, such as they were, were interrupted by the sudden death of his father, and he left Cambridge without a degree and at 18 became responsible for the care of his mother and sisters.

Tradition maintains he then went to Lincoln's Inn to study law, but his admitted distaste for academic work makes this questionable. It is known he was in London when he was 20, and it was while he was in the capital that he met and married Elizabeth Bourchier, the daughter of a wealthy leather merchant, two years older than himself.

He returned to live at Huntingdon and to take up his responsibilities as head of the family. Between 1623 and 1629 he and Elizabeth had five children. His income was barely sufficient to maintain his family, and his formerly rich uncle at Hinchingbrooke was rich no more. He had lavishly entertained monarchs hoping for rewards. These had not come and he had been forced to sell Hinchingbrooke. Cromwell became an MP for Huntingdon in 1628 and watched from the wings the growing rift between the king and his parliament. As his financial problems increased, he sold his land at Huntingdon for £1,800 and for a time contemplated a new life in America. Whether or not be took this idea seriously it is difficult to say, but in the event he landed up not in New England but in St Ives.

He was now severely short of money. He had no land and had to rent a farm. This he did north of Market Hill and probably moved with his family into Old Slepe Hall. This was situated in the area where Cromwell Terrace and Cromwell Place now stand. There is no way of knowing exactly where the house was, but it seems likely it was on the east side near where a dental surgery is now located. When the houses were being built in the last century, workmen excavating the sites stumbled upon a cellar stocked with bottles of elder wine which probably belonged to Cromwell. The workmen enjoyed an afternoon tasting what they had found and afterwards reported the wine to be sweet, thick and syrupy. In 1636 an uncle, Sir Thomas Steward, died and left Oliver Cromwell a large estate at Ely. From that point the St Ives farmer had no more financial problems.

Cromwell's arrival in St Ives appears to have coincided with a drastic change in the aimless type of life he had hitherto led. He became known for his devoutness and for the simple manner in which he and his family lived. The historian Brayley writes: "his success in his new business was altogether impeded through the loss of time which he and his servants daily consumed in prayer, and other devotional exercises".

There is one signature in the vestry book of All Saints still in existence and he is said to have paid the churchwardens five shillings for some willows, but there is no record of that transaction. The people of St Ives soon got used to the quiet, earnest figure of the farmer strolling their streets. They also grew accustomed to the site of his muscular figure in church as he bent over his pew deep in prayer. He invariably wore a red flannel scarf around his neck as he was subject to sore throats.

There is no doubt that the five years he spent in St Ives formed a very important part in Cromwell's life. The king was already in dispute with his parliament and many people, particularly the puritans, were becoming increasingly annoyed with what they considered the monarch's arrogance and disdain for anything his opponents advocated. As he went about his daily work and sought inspiration in prayer, he must have wondered how it would all end. Perhaps the seeds of his republicanism were sown as he strolled by the river on his way to All Saints.

Cromwell would have worshipped in the parish church with many others who objected to the signs of popery they noticed in the services. St Ives already had a strong nonconformist tradition, and Cromwell would have seen eye to eye with many of his fellow worshippers. One of these was a man who was to scandalise many devout parishioners by a bequest he left when he died. Dr Robert Wilde, a doctor of divinity and a man with strong puritanical tendencies, was 22 when Cromwell came to farm the acres bordering the town. Perhaps the two men chatted as they left the church together, the learned doctor brooding on the evils of the papacy and the farmer pondering the future of parliamentary government and the iniquities of the Stuarts. One was to go down in his nation's history. The other was to leave to St Ives a curious and controversial legacy.

Cromwell kept a close eye on what was happening in London while he lived at St Ives, but most of his time was spent in running his farm. Several noted writers have referred to this period of his life. Thomas Carlyle notes: "He was a man studious of many temporal and many eternal things. His cattle grazed here, his plough tilled here. The heavenly skies and infernal abysses overarched and underarched him here".

Carlyle went on to say: "Oliver's life at St Ives and Ely, as a sober, industrious farmer, is it not altogether as that of a true and devout man? He has renounced the world and its ways – its prizes are not the things that can enrich him. He tills the earth; he reads his bible; daily assembles his servants round him to worship God. His main hopes, I do believe, were fixed on the Higher World; and his aim to get well thither, by walking well through his humble course in this world".

Foster in his *Lives of the Statesmen of the Commonwealth*, declares: "In the care of the St Ives farm, he now not only sought employment for some portion of his ill-subdued energy, which always craved in him for action, but also put to proof the value of the thoughts we have attributed to him. . . . He achieved an influence through the neighbourhood all round him unequalled for piety and self denying virtue. The greater part of his time, even upon his farm, was passed in devotional exercises, expositions and prayers. Who prays best will work best. Who preaches best will fight best. All the famous doctrines of his later and more celebrated years were tried and tested on the little farm at St Ives".

Cromwell took a lively interest in local politics and Noble says it is clear that he was not on good terms with the established church in St Ives. He did, though, worship regularly at All Saints. There are two entries in the vestry minutes, both relating to the appointment of parish officers, with which he was concerned. In one entry his signature has been removed, apparently by a churchwarden in 1732. In the other his signature can be seen alongside that of nine other parishioners.

When Cromwell moved to Ely, his financial problems were solved once and for all. He was in the cathedral city when the Civil War started in 1642, and from then on his rise was meteoric. He had raised a troop of horse, and soon he was a cavalry colonel. Before long he was made lieutenant general and put in charge of the parliamentary cavalry in East Anglia.

It was while he was harassing royalist forces in this region that he probably had a say in the decision to break the town's bridge. Bob Burn-Murdoch, curator of the Norris Museum, explains why this was done in his book, *St Ives Bridge and Chapel*, published in 1988. In 1643 the Roundhead forces at Cambridge feared a royalist attack, and the town was packed with Parliamentary troops. Among them was Cromwell, then a colonel, and also Cambridge's MP. The king's army, however, retreated westward and the Parliamentary forces dispersed, leaving Cromwell in charge of a small garrison.

The energetic colonel ranged as far afield as Lowestoft and King's Lynn, but at the back of his mind there lurked the thought that if the king ever did launch a major attack into East Anglia, bridges such as those at Huntingdon and St Ives, would assume enormous strategic importance. Both Cambridge and St Ives were left in peace for a while, but Cromwell had probably already realised what must be done if either town came under threat.

The threat materialised two years later when King Charles made a lightning dash down the Great North Road from Yorkshire, seized Huntingdon and plundered it. Although he withdrew again, the Roundheads had been alarmed, and with a royalist stronghold still holding out at Newark, they decided the bridge at St Ives must be broken. In coming to this decision they might well have consulted the commander who, they knew, was familiar with the area.

It was either the southernmost arch or the one next to it that was shattered, and a drawbridge substituted. It was not repaired until 1716 when the Duke of Manchester had the bridge restored to its original design. Edmund Pettis the eighteenth-century St Ives diarist noted the event. In a brief entry in his diary he recorded: "1716. The two arches next ye Dolphen of the great bridge rebuilt from ye foundation by CM". CM was Charles, Earl of Manchester, whose family owned the manor of St Ives. After the Dissolution of the monasteries, ownership of the town passed through several hands, and in 1628 it was sold to the first Earl of Manchester. It was the fourth earl, who was created a duke in 1719, who restored the bridge. The manor remained in the possession of the Manchester family until the 1920s. The second duke carried on his father's work, for in 1722 Pettis wrote: "The bridg sett by Wm D of Manchester with pible", which presumably means that the duke had paved the road over the bridge with cobblestones. These were replaced with granite setts in the last century. The road is now tarmacadamed.

Oliver Cromwell was elected Lord Protector on December 12, 1653, and went to live at Westminister. He took with him his aged mother who had always lavished all her affection on her only son. She was given apartments in Whitehall where she lived until her death in 1654. She reluctantly took part in the pageantry of Whitehall, but was not dazzled by the splendour of her son's surroundings. Noble writes: "The regard she had for Oliver, rendered her constantly wretched from the apprehension she had of his danger; she was discontented if she did not see him twice a day, and never heard the report of a gun but she exclaimed: 'my son is shot'". On her death bed she asked for a private funeral, but her son ordered a solemn public burial in Westminster Abbey. After the Restoration her body was dug up and thrown with others into a grave dug in St Margaret's churchyard.

Cromwell himself died in his bed at Whitehall on September 3, 1658. It was the eighth anniversary of his triumph at Dunbar and the seventh anniversary of his great victory at Worcester. He was buried with regal pomp in Westminster Abbey, but after the return of Charles II his body was dug up and exposed upon the gallows at Tyburn. Later the trunk was thrown into a hole beneath the gallows and the head set up on a pole outside Westminster Hall.

The royalist members of the family meanwhile, were busy reverting to the name of Williams, realising that the name Cromwell would not go down well at the court of Charles II. One member of the family was to die a curious death due to a heady mixture of election fever and alcohol. This Williams had nominated a candidate for a by-election at Huntingdon, and his man was opposed by a candidate selected by the Earl of Manchester. According to Noble: "The contest was carried out with extreme violence, exceeding everything of that kind that had happened there; several lives were lost amongst the mobs of both parties. Mr Williams' friend lost it, and he, indulging himself too freely in liquor after the election was over, died immediately". Tradition has it that Williams was sitting drinking with friends in a Huntingdon hotel when he was told the result. He is said to have slumped forward in his chair and died. His death took place on 3rd August 1673 and he was buried at Ramsey.

It was two and a half centuries after his death before a statue to Cromwell was raised in St Ives. This omission had been noted with surprise by several well known politicians and Lord John Russell who, for a brief period sat as one of Huntingdon's MPs, once remarked: "The only great man the shire has produced, and what he did for England and the world is rightly deemed the grandest of all their local associations, but they have not yet dared to raise a statue to his honour on the soil from which he sprang".

Fig. 9. The statue of Oliver Cromwell in the Market Hill, St Ives; unveiled in 1901 and recently cleaned and restored.

Many years after Russell made this remark, a move was made in Huntingdon to commission a statue. The public were asked to supply the money, but after an early burst of enthusiasm, it became evident that the residents of the town in which the Protector was born were not really interested in the idea. Back in 1849 subscriptions were being sought in St Ives. Money was coming in steadily, but a year later the Rev. E. Paxton Hood of Ramsey published a poem commemorating Cromwell which glowed with such Roundhead fervour that it offended many people in the town. One of its verses read:

> Raise up, raise up the pillar, some grand old granite stone,
> To the king without a sceptre, to the prince without a throne,
> To the brave old English hero who broke our feudal gyves,
> To the leader of the good old cause – the farmer of St Ives.

The scheme was abandoned, and in 1899, exactly three hundred years after the birth of Cromwell, Huntingdon decided it would not have a statue. At this point interest was renewed in St Ives, and this time the money was forthcoming and the statue was commissioned.

It was sculpted in London by F. W. Pomeroy and, before being brought to St Ives, was exhibited at the Royal Academy where it won considerable acclaim. Cromwell is cast in bronze and his dress is in keeping with that of a farmer of St Ives rather than that of a victorious general or ruler of England. Frozen forever in statuary, he looks out towards the east on Market Hill, a sword buckled by his side and a bible under his right arm. His hand is held out as if in mute appeal to passers-by to remove the Cross of Sacrifice standing ahead of him straight in front of his immobilised eyes. The statue stands on a pedestal of York Stone.

The unveiling ceremony in 1901 divided the town. Civic dignitaries were present and flags flew from windows, but there were large gaps where residents shut their windows and tried to pretend nothing out of the ordinary was going on in the town centre. Several prominent St Ivians shunned the ceremony. There were no vocal protests or demonstrations, but the police thwarted an attempt by local Jacobites to throw nooses into the crowd. Cromwell enthusiasts packed the market square and, after the statue had been unveiled, repaired to the Corn Exchange for a magnificent lunch.

The menu for this lunch says a good deal about civic hospitality at the turn of the century. Today most meals hosted by local government authorities are spartan affairs. Those attending the unveiling of Cromwell's statue were confronted with this menu:

> Lobster Mayonnaise.
> Roast and Baked Chickens, York Ham, Tongue, Roast Beef,
> Braised Beef, Veal and Ham Pies, Pigeon Pies, Roast
> and Boiled Turkeys, Pheasants, Galantine of Veal.
> Fruit Tarts. Cream. Trifles. Blancmange. Pineapple Jellies.
> Pastry.
> Cheese. Celery.

What the "prince without a throne" would have thought of such extravagance makes interesting conjecture.

From time to time Cromwell suffers indignities. On Friday or Saturday nights inebriated youths once in a while risk their lives by climbing the statue to place utensils on the Protector's head, but generally the statue is a respected feature of the town. After the chapel on the bridge, it is probably the most photographed landmark of St Ives.

Chapter 7
A Mischievous Puritan

One of Oliver Cromwell's contemporaries during the time he resided in St Ives was the curate of All Saints, a cheerful little doctor of divinity, who shared with the earnest farmer a dislike of the doctrines of Rome. Dr Robert Wilde was a highly intelligent minister with an impish sense of humour whose name is recalled in the parish church once a year to this day. It is because of his legacy that once every year children cast dice before the altar of the church trying to win bibles.

Little is known of the man who bequeathed such an odd tradition to the town in which he was born and in which he served his parishioners for several years. The only surviving account of him comes from a subsequent curate who was at All Saints in the last century. Dr John Hunt served under one vicar for a number of years, and was promptly dismissed by that vicar's successor. This peremptory dismissal is not all that surprising when one considers what sort of man Hunt was. After he left St Ives he wrote a highly entertaining account of his life there, full of amusing, even wicked insights into life at the vicarage. A clever man with a sharp, barbed tongue, he must have been a difficult curate.

Robert Wilde was a poet as well as being a man of the cloth, and during his lifetime he wrote many poems some of which achieved a good deal of popularity. Hunt must have heard of him, because after he left St Ives, he took the trouble of making a collection of Wilde's poems. He had these privately published in book form, and in 1870 sent a copy to his St Ives friend, Read Adams, a churchwarden at All Saints. Hunt admits the poems are not among the best Wilde wrote, and his account of Wilde is sketchy and interspersed with chunks of local history, but it is the only account we have.

Wilde was born in the town in 1609 and, according to Hunt, it became obvious at an early age that he had the makings of a first-rate poet. But he was impelled by a desire to enter the church even though he soon began to have misgivings about certain aspects of doctrine. Hunt writes: "Of all the counties in England, Huntingdon is the most theological. The people never tire of religious discussion. The whole county is only 29 miles in length and 22 in breadth, but the part it has borne in ecclesiastical history, and the interest it has taken in church controversies, make it not the least of the tribes of Israel. The theological spirit is hereditary. Huntingdonshire is described in old history as without gentry. The property was in the hands of the religious houses".

Wilde would have been a young man of 22 when Cromwell arrived in St Ives and they may well have become friends. The volatile minister and the ponderous farmer would have shared many views. In particular, they would have been united in opposing what they saw as creeping papacy within the established church. Religion was a constant theme of conversation in the town, for as Hunt says: "There is perhaps no town in England where Dissent is so strong as it is in St Ives".

Wilde's poems were originally published and sold on sheets which can still be seen in the British Museum. In 1670 they were re-published in one volume. Hunt says they enjoyed great popularity in London. He quotes Dryden as saying Wilde was particularly liked in the capital where "the citizens bought more editions of his works than would lie under all the pies at the Lord Mayor's Christmas". Dryden went on to say: "I have seen them reading it in the midst of 'Change time nay, so vehemently were they at it, that they lost their bargains by the candles' ends". He added that the poems were equally well received by high born and educated people.

A sure sign of this popularity emerged after Wilde's death when many mediocre poems were published by unknown authors in his name. There were so many of these that Wilde's reputation was in danger of becoming tarnished. Hunt admits that some of the poems in his collection were not of much value and may not have been written by Wilde.

Two of the shortest poems in Hunt's collection are epitaphs. One is for a good man, the other for a wicked one. The first reads:

> Here lies a piece of Christ, a star in dust,
> A vein of gold, a china dish that must
> Be used in Heaven, when God shall feast the just.

The second epitaph declares:

> Here lies the carcass of a cursèd sinner,
> Doomed to be roasted for the devil's dinner.

The minister had a keen wit and was apt to scandalise listeners with some of his remarks. On one occasion after he had applied for the living at Ayhno in Northamptonshire and knew there was a rival applicant, he was asked by a serious minded colleague whether he had got the ministry. He replied: "We have divided it. I have got the 'aye', and he has got the 'no'" One contemporary described him as "a fat, jolly and boon presbyterian". Another writer talks about him as "generous, free-hearted, jolly, witty and facetious", adding: "All of which qualities do very rarely or seldom meet in men of the presbyterian persuasion, who generally are morose, clownish and of sullen and reserved nature". A facetious, jolly Puritan was certainly the antithesis of the popular image of members of that staid religion.

Hunt himself takes up this point. "The Puritans were not all sad", be observes. Dr Wilde had a gushing, joyful nature. It was born in him and it was only to the outward appearance that it seemed to conflict with the seriousness of mind which his profession required. On one occasion Wilde was rebuked by one of his superiors for displaying too much levity. This cleric told him it detracted from his dignity as a minister. Some time later this same man came to listen to one of Wilde's sermons and afterwards went up to express his regret at his earlier remarks. Wilde was also known for his strict temperance and sobriety. "He was very serious in serious things", one friend recalled after Wilde's death. He died at Oundle in 1679 aged 70.

The legacy that this rubicund cleric who was "very serious in serious things" left to St Ives led to a unique service being held once a year in All Saints. With his known puritanical views he would naturally have disliked some of the practices of the Anglican church. He would also have been against anything that he would have regarded as "frippery" in the surroundings of the services. He would not have liked statues, nor stained glass windows. The lofty spire of the parish church would not have met with his approval, and he certainly would not have willingly gone up to the altar to receive communion. This was a practice with which no dissenter agreed. Dissenters argued that it interrupted a worshipper's devotions and meditations. The minister should bring the communion bread down into the body of the church so each member of the congregation could receive it in his pew.

Wilde's sense of humour must have been active when he put his signature to his will in 1675. He intended to show from beyond the grave his abhorrence of the altar by turning it once a year into a gaming table.

After leaving some bequests to various members of his family, Wilde stated that he was leaving £50 to the church to be administered by the vicar and churchwardens. The money was to be used to buy a plot of land which would yield an income of £3 each year. Each year at Whitsun 12 children, six boys and six girls, were then to be chosen to cast dice.

These children had all to be: 1. "Such as are good and of good report; 2. all born in the parish; 3. each above the age of 12 years; and 4 everyone able to read the Bible". In the

Fig. 10. Bible Dicing in All Saints' church, May 1989. The contest is watched by (*left to right*) Mrs Carole Everall, deputy mayoress; Rev. David Moore, vicar of All Saints; and Cllr Mrs Jean Chandler, deputy mayor.

meantime the minister and the churchwardens were to use the income from the land to buy "six plain and well bound bibles in English, never exceeding seven shillings each".

The will went on: "Upon the Whitsun Tuesday before morning prayer, after the sermon bell is rung, the minister and officers and other grave townsmen being also present, the minister in a few words praying to God to direct the lots to His glory, let a saucer with three dice be prepared upon the table, and, beginning with the males, let one bible be cast for by each pair, and the party who casts the greater number at one cast have that bible, and so two by two until all be cast for". It is clear that the table referred to was the altar, and this horrified many local Christians who claimed that Wilde was mocking God.

The service, which still takes place each year, continued to be highly controversial right up to the present century. It is no longer regarded as shocking. In the years following Wilde's death the service caused considerable controversy in the town and the surrounding villages. The service was, however, defended by some nonconformist ministers.

In 1713 the sermon at the gaming service was preached by the Rev Simon Ockley, Professor of Arabic at Cambridge University, and chaplain to the Earl of Oxford. He also appears to have been vicar of Swavesey. Professor Ockley told his congregation: "A great many persons have censured the disposing of the bibles by throwing of a dice as being not only whimsical but exceedingly indecent, especially considering it is done in a church. I desire such, whenever they should find themselves so piously disposed of as to leave anything towards the buying of books of religion and devotion for those who are not able to purchase them for themselves, to oblige the world with the invention of a better way of casting lots".

The professor was voicing a minority opinion, and ministers, and later the Press, continued to rail against the service for the next two centuries. As late as 1897 one local newspaper told its readers: "Many strange things were done in olden times, but at this late period of the nineteenth century, every reasonable person will agree that such a ridiculous custom as this should speedily be put an end to".

Until well into this century the land which the churchwardens of All Saints bought with Wilde's £50 was known as Bible Orchard. It is now the site of the town's library. Over the years the dicing has been moved from the altar and has taken place in various parts of the church. One vicar insisted on it taking place as close as possible to the door leading into the church. Today the gaming is done on a plain wooden table in front of the altar.

Many vicars have been offended by having to take the service, but none has refused to do so. The attitude of the present minister, the softly-spoken David Moore, was disclosed at a recent service. "Here we are dicing for bibles, and in a church", he told his congregation. "What a strange business it is, is it not? But never mind, it is a bit of history, and, so long as it is treated as a bit of innocent fun, there is no harm in it". The Rev Moore's predecessor, Canon Ronald Jennings, now living in retirement in Lincolnshire, also had no scruples about holding the service. He says he met few parishioners who objected strongly to it.

There has been no major change over the years in the form of service, but some things have altered. Wilde who nursed throughout his life a hatred for Catholicism, would have detested one feature of today's service. Instead of the original dozen children casting dice each year, there are now two dozen gambling for 12 bibles. Wilde had envisaged Anglican children dicing annually forever, but over the years as nonconformist churches were established and thrived in St Ives, the rules were changed to include Methodists and members of the Free Church congregations.

By 1970, 18 children from three congregations were taking part. In that year the Roman Catholics asked to be included and, since 1971, 24 children, six from each of the four major churches, stand a chance of winning one of Wilde's bibles. It is this last change which would have appalled the man who bequeathed one of the most curious church services in the land to All Saints.

Chapter 8
Three Chroniclers

St Ives has been fortunate in that over the past 300 years it has produced a trio of local chroniclers deeply interested in the events that took place in their home town during their lifetimes. In the eighteenth century Edmund Pettis, a shopkeeper and small farmer, was an obsessive notetaker and carefully recorded what he observed. In the next century John Skeeles, a builder, left his account of what he had seen, and finally Herbert Norris, founder of the local museum, brought the record up to 1930.

The first two had no thought of writing for posterity. Their diaries were a consuming hobby to be shown only to relatives and close friends. The style in which they wrote makes this clear. Both Pettis and Skeeles would be amazed to know that their writings are now kept in the Norris Museum and are referred to by modern day researchers.

Norris was by far the most literate of the three and throughout his life fostered an ambition to make a significant contribution to the historical record of the county he loved. A lonely, aloof, and in many ways a frustrated man, he spent a lifetime collecting books, records and stray memorabilia relating to Huntingdonshire.

Although born in St Ives, Norris spent his working life in the Gloucestershire town of Cirencester. A jeweller, he became friendly while still a young man with another jeweller in Cambridge who had west country connections. Norris bought a jewellery shop in Cirencester where he lived in a large house in which he housed his growing collection. A bachelor, this collection soon became an obsession with him, and as it grew, it was said that he would have his socks and shirts lying about the house because he was filling cupboards and drawers with more and more items.

He never lost his love for his home county and made regular visits to St Ives where his cousin Fred ran a boot and shoe shop in Crown Street. His sister Emily was also a shopkeeper next door to her brother, and presided over a children's wear and fancy goods store. Norris spent his holidays in St Ives relentlessly pursuing his hobby of collecting information. Elderly people still living in the town who knew him, recall that he was a fastidious, highly organised man. A remote figure, he rarely went out socially, had few close friends and could be a prickly character. At some stage he decided that when he retired he would settle down in Huntingdonshire and in due course bought Ferrar House in Huntingdon for a retirement home.

It is only by a twist of fate that the Norris Museum is located in St Ives. All the evidence points to the fact that Norris intended it to be in Ferrar House after his death. His collection in Cirencester had been carefully catalogued and looked after by his housekeeper, Elsie Pope, and from what he told friends, it is evident that he wished the collection to be transferred to Huntingdon before he died.

Norris intended to make a will to this effect, a will in which he also meant to make financial provision for his sister, now ageing. He died rather suddenly in March 1931 without making this will. It was then discovered that in a will drawn up in 1903, he had left his collection to the town of St Ives. In this will he bequeathed only £250 to his sister. This faced St Ives Council, which then had borough status, with a problem.

It finally decided to look for a suitable building to serve as a museum and to transfer Norris' collection to St Ives. The council then bought the property owned by carpenter and

Fig. 11. Herbert Norris (1859–1931), historian of St Ives and founder of the Norris Museum.

boat builder Henry Gore, whose fondness for alcohol had got him into financial difficulties. The building was virtually rebuilt and Norris' collection was brought to St Ives. Elsie Pope agreed to move to the town, was appointed librarian and moved into the house.

Members of the council were conscious that they had a moral obligation to do something for Emily Norris. They took legal advice to see if they could give her an annual income, but this was not possible. Instead they appointed her as a paid secretary. The museum was opened in 1933.

In 1889 Norris had published a History of St Ives. It was by no means comprehensive, nor did the author intend it be. It ran to 96 pages and was written almost in note form, a fact which Norris acknowledged in a preface. He wrote that he had used the word "history" in the title, but that his work "should have been named Notes contributed towards a History of St Ives". In another sentence he discloses his secret desire to write something more substantial. "My purpose in contributing the articles", he said, "was to get my information into a handy form for future work and private reference, in the hope that I might ultimately contribute something of importance towards the History of Huntingdonshire, a work I am much interested in, and am now engaged upon". That sentence contains Norris' sad secret. To the day of his death he was working on what he hoped would be an authoritative history.

All three chroniclers are reliable when talking about events they witnessed. None of them can really be trusted when they refer to historical events. Pettis is probably the least reliable in this respect. His references to Oliver Cromwell at times border on the comic. Obviously an arch-royalist who would happily have given his life for the royalist cause on a battlefield, Pettis believed the most scurrilous reports which were widely circulated after the Protector's death. But he is entirely trustworthy when he writes about things he actually saw.

The Pettis Manuscript runs to 100 pages, but only 24 pages are devoted to chronicle. The author's real passion lay in meticulously recording the rural scene around St Ives in the eighteenth century. Page after page of his manuscript is devoted to exquisitely drawn maps of fields and meadows. In his neat handwriting he has written down the names of landowners and tenants, together with the amount of land each individual held. The maps are lovingly executed, but today hold only a passing interest to the casual museum visitor. As an accurate portrait of a small rural town in the early 1700s, the maps are priceless.

Pettis took a keen interest in the weather and many of his entries refer to it. Under the heading Remarkable Observations he writes about the winter of 1683: "November 17th set in a great frost and froz night and day, so sevear that working ceased for some time till people's bodies were seasoned unto it, Then went on again. Yet still it continued to an extream, not abundance of snow not much wind but thick rimes for many days and nights continuance . . . with a very sevear keen air. Thus it continued to 23rd December when it thawed a little which gave hope twas going but proved a mistake . . . For it freeze again as vemant as ever. Twas very troublesome to presarve any bear and as hard to get water for cattel – all ponds, brooks, and rivers being locked so fast that loaden cartes could go almost anywhere. Thus it continued with little or no abatement till the 20th of Feb when it began to thaw gradual and without much rain".

On May 3rd 1699 the town suffered a blizzard with more snow falling the next day. Pettis continues his climatic notes: "On November 26th 1703 at nine at night arose a violent wind which blew extream all night, at six next morning was the most terrible gust as ever was known, which did abundance of damage at sea and land". The storm was apparently nationwide as he goes on to say: "The Bishop of Bath and his lady were killed by the fall of chimnys at their bed. Likewise many were killed in London by fall of chimnys, some blown down in this town". August 6th 1707 witnessed a heatwave so intense all harvesting was stopped at 10am. Pettis records that the day was dubbed "Hot Wensday".

Pettis gives us the only authentic account of the fire which engulfed St Ives in April 1689. The account is brief but colourful. He writes: "Hear happened a sudden and dreadful fire in a malt house at the end of White Hart Lane next padlemore (a paddock near the present Greyhound public house). The wind being very high it ran up to the street, flew cross the sheep market consuming all to the riverside with part of the Bridg Street and to the other side of the bridg consumed part of them two houses. It laid in ashes several innes, messuages (yards and outbuildings) and dwelling places belonging to 122 persons and families together with their houshold goods, malt, corn, grain, hay, shopgoods, wares, and marchantdizes. The damage amounting to upwards of £13,072.

    Towards this loss:
        Come in by voluntary contribution   £2,066.11. 4½.
        Collected by brief   £1,478. 5.10½.

                                                                                      £3,544.17. 3".

The "brief" he refers to was a "disaster message" which was sent to all neighbouring parishes and was then circulated throughout the country appealing for funds.

Pettis witnessed and played a prominent part in the town's celebrations marking Queen Anne's coronation in April 1702. The day started with the ringing of church bells. There was music played in the streets and people in festive mood went from door to door drinking and generally enjoying themselves. At 11am Pettis tells us: "I formed a cavelcade in the courtyard west of the church which made a gallant appearance". The procession then made its way to the sheep market where a whole ox had been roasted and cut up. There were also cakes and other food for the residents. The canopy at the head of the procession had been "artfully made, very rich and fine. A table on the market stood on a fine carpet and it was covered with fine damask. On the table stood a crown studded with jewels". The festivities lasted all day and well into the night.

It was at about this time that local newspapers began appearing regularly and Pettis mentions this fact. St Ives was the home of three newspapers published before 1722 – the *St Ives Post*, March 1716 or 1717, lasted until 1718, the *St Ives Postboy* established in 1718 and the *St Ives Mercury* which first came out some time in 1719.

Robert Raikes set up a printing press in the town in 1718 when the population was very small, and may have thought that buying a paper already established was the best way to do it. His family came from Yorkshire. In 1718 he was working for a printer in York when he decided to move south to St Ives where the *Post* was already established and was being printed by J. Fisher.

It lasted only about 15 months and was succeeded by the *Postboy*, issued by Raikes who appears to have bought Fisher out. This was still being published in 1719 when Raikes went into partnership with William Dicey and brought out the *Mercury*. Only one edition of this newspaper, the sixth, has survived. It was dated 16th November 1719. Dicey, whose family were to be connected with journalism and printing for more than 150 years, was the son of Thomas Dicey, born about 1660, who built up a lucrative business selling "quack" medicines in the Fens. Tradition had it that William hit upon the idea of using the men who peddled these dubious pills and potions around the countryside to distribute newspapers as well. It is known that the *Mercury* was still appearing early in 1720, but reference to it disappears after that date. Raikes and Dicey, perhaps recognising that a town the size of St Ives could not support a newspaper, looked for another town offering more scope. Dicey settled for Northampton and, in May 1720, published the first edition of the *Northampton Mercury*. Raikes moved to Gloucester to start the *Gloucester Journal*.

Pettis says of the disappearance of the *St Ives Mercury* that the paper "chanced to print something that did not suit the times nor please a certain Knight, who brought him (Raikes) under prosecution and fine". The "certain Knight" was probably Sir Edward Lawrence,

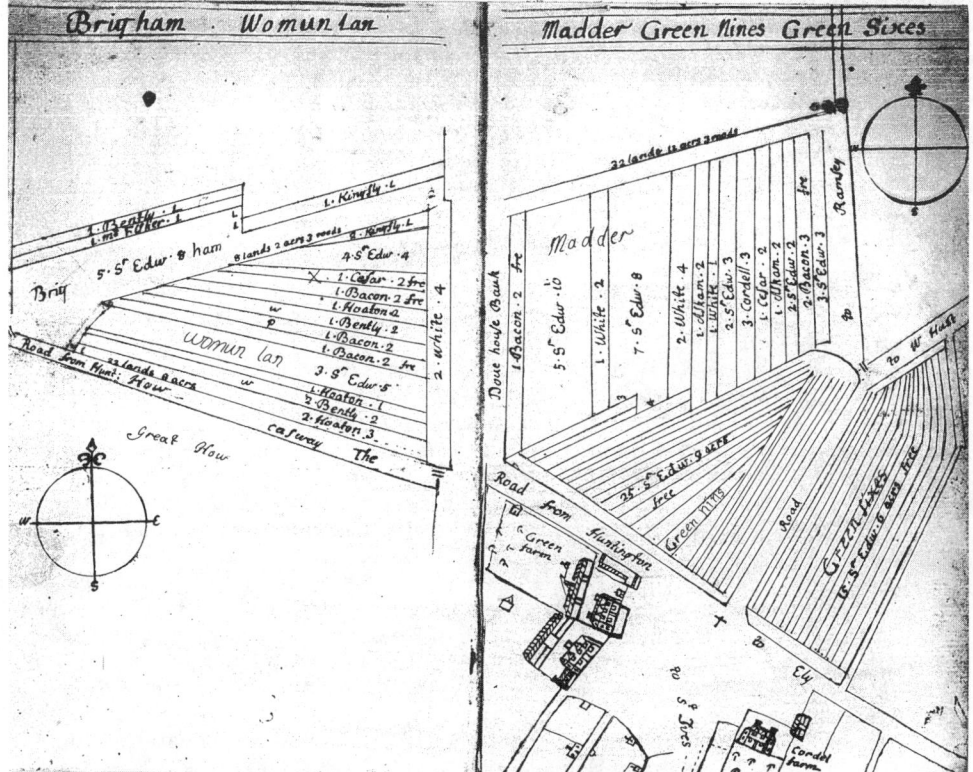

Fig. 12. The Norris Museum (*above*), and an extract from the Edmund Pettis manuscript, showing land around the junction of Houghton Road and Ramsey Road.

owner of Cromwell's former home Old Slepe Hall, and the biggest landowner in St Ives apart from the Duke of Manchester.

Pettis was apparently a religious man, as he records many church events, most of them trivial. A substantial part of the chronicle concerns Oliver Cromwell and it is when we come to these passages that we must not take them too seriously. Pettis' historical reflections are highly unreliable. He obviously read extensively, but the books he chose to read appeared to be those which fitted in with his own preconceived ideas. His references to Oliver Cromwell are particularly suspect. Letters he copies were evidently contained in a book written by an author who favoured the Stuarts. All are certainly fictitious, and his account of the Protector selling his soul to the devil is regarded by serious historians today as bordering on the hilarious.

One set of letters concerns an exchange between Cromwell and Hugh Peters, a Cornish puritan divine, who emigrated to Holland and then to New England. He returned to this country in 1641, a year before the Civil War broke out, and became army chaplain.

In a letter supposed to have been written shortly before the execution of Charles I, Peters addressed Cromwell as "Champion of the Lord," and says: "an unexpressible exultation of joy incites me to congratulate you who hath so often exposed yr precious life in fighting of the Lord of Hosts battles, upon seeing this happy day wherein we have totally subdued and taken prisoner that Grand Tyrant of the earth, Charles Stuart. To make good this text, bind their kings with chains and their nobles with fetters of iron . . . the Lord direct you for the best in all your councils and in the mean time I am proud of being in your favour".

Cromwell reacted to this effusion by replying that he had received it "joyfully". He went on to discuss the position of the captive king because of whom "we had fire and sword devouring us in every corner of the land. So that he must expect that with what measure he meated it, shall be measured to him again".

In January 1649 Cromwell again wrote to Peters addressing him as "Friend of my Bosom". He wrote: "I greatly rejoice to see this blessed day wherein we completed the work of the Lord in condemning the wicked Charles Stuart to dy for his manifold transgressions. I believe it is evidently known to you and to all that espouse our righteous cause, how great an instrument I was in subduing the tyrant.

"But then it was by such means which will seem no less strange to you than somewhat uneasy to me. But as I can trust you with the secret which I conjure you never to reveal to any, I must confess to you that when I first entered upon a military employment to relieve my injured country from oppression, the day after I received my commission, walking in the evening in Hyde Park, the Devil appeared to me in human shape and upon promises of assuring me always success over my enemies, the honour thereof tempted me to sell my soul and body to him. But not to take possession thereof till the expiration of thirty nine years commencing from the day and date of our contract. But though he has punctually observed his articles on his part (yet it is my opinion and I also desire yours in your next letter), that I am not in conscience bound to stand to my obligation because the cause which I fought for was not his, for he encourages popery, tyranny, arbitrary power and wicked princes. Therefore the contract is null and voyd. But let it be as it will I desire your advice in it and in the mean time I rest the true and constant hearer of your soul saving doctrine".

The preacher replied saying Cromwell's secret would die with him. He went on: "what you have done in defence of our cause is allowable and praiseworthy. For had you as many souls and bodies as you have men under your command, the bargain for which you sold them was worth the price". Peters went on to assure his friend: "Satan has no power over you because he was the occasion of all that bloodshed by our enemies and encouraged them to ruin and destroy our country".

This is the last we hear in Pettis of Peters who was hung, drawn and quartered after the Restoration. He was not an attractive man, but he met his end manfully. C. V. Wedgwood in her *Trial of Charles I*, writes "Hugh Peters was perhaps the most to be pitied. It was true that he had exulted in the king's death, but he had really done nothing to procure it. Bustling about in a state of enthusiasm and preaching ferocious sermons do not amount to murder. At his trial a great deal of play was made with the popular fable that he himself had been the executioner. This he denied. But he had no hope of acquittal. He had been too deeply engaged with the regicides, and he had become to many a symbol of the hypocritical zealous saint".

Pettis appears fascinated with Oliver Cromwell. Commenting on the correspondence between the Protector and Peters, he writes: "By these letters and all their canting, it plainly appears that this fanatical crew used all possible means in the whole course of their proceedings by vile insinuations to cheat the people. So now you see how they are trying likewise to trick the devil too, by a little quirk in law as they thought.

"It was in 1644 that Oliver received his commission fron Parliament and had another immediately from the devil and pleased both masters which he knew was possible because they were Men and Devils. This compact was made to answer his ambitious, aspiring heart that so much thirsted after honour though to the loss of his soul".

Pettis recounts another story alleging that Cromwell sold his soul to Satan in return for the promise of triumph on the field of battle. Many versions of this story were embellished, printed and openly sold after Cromwell's death. Pettis' version is brief and patchy, and a more detailed, colourful account was printed in pamphlet form in 1720 and sold at The Angel in Paternoster Row by a Mr Boreham.

The author claims it is a record of an incident witnessed by Colonel Lindsey, a first captain of Cromwell's regiment of horse. Lindsey claims that shortly before the decisive Parliamentary victory over the Royalist forces at the battle of Worcester on September 3, 1651, Cromwell took him to a wood not far from where his army was encamped. The two men dismounted and Cromwell ordered his companion to follow him into the forest and to note carefully all he saw and heard.

After they had gone a little way into the wood Lindsey, who might well have become uneasy about the reason for this odd stroll, cried out that he was feeling ill and did not know why. Cromwell asked him what the matter was and his junior replied he was "in such a trembling and consternation, that he never felt the like in all the conflicts and battles he had engaged in. But whether it proceeded from the gloominess of the place or the temperament of his body I know not".

Cromwell dismissed it as a fit of the vapours and ordered Lindsey to keep following his commander. After they had gone only a few more yards, Lindsey was rooted to the ground and cried out in terror that he was unable to move. Cromwell derided him for being "a faint hearted fool", and said the colonel should remain where he was and witness what was about to happen. According to Lindsey, Cromwell walked on and saw a grave, elderly man approaching him, carrying a roll of parchment. Lindsey later said he was so astonished, his curiosity overcame his terror, and he remained a silent witness. Cromwell took the parchment and read it carefully. The colonel then heard a heated argument and heard Cromwell exclaim: "this is but for seven years. I was to have had it for one and twenty, and it must and shall be so . . .".

The old man insisted it could only be for seven years, and when Cromwell attempted to bargain for 14, remained obdurate, remarking that if Cromwell were not willing to take the contract up, there were many other men who would. Cromwell finally accepted the document and rejoined Lindsey "with great joy in his countenance". This was something that quite evidently was not lighting up Lindsey's face when he rode back to the camp with Cromwell, who was now itching to engage the Royalists as soon as possible. By now the colonel had already decided to desert at the earliest possible opportunity. After the first charge, Lindsey took advantage of the confusion to slip away from the field and to ride with all speed to the house of a friend, the Rev. Thorowgood in Norfolk.

When the minister saw Lindsey ride into his yard breathless and covered in dust, he greeted him with the query: "we hear there is likely to be a battle shortly. What, fled from your colours?" Lindsey confirmed a battle had already taken place and that he felt the king must have been defeated. He added: "If ever I strike a stroak for Cromwell again, may I perish eternally for I am sure he has made a league with the devil, and the devil will have him in due time".

He then recounted all the circumstances leading to his desertion. He ended by saying he was convinced Cromwell would "certainly die seven years that day the battle was fought". Cromwell did die on the seventh anniversary of the battle of Worcester. This coincidence probably fired the imaginations of fervent royalist writers. Reports that Cromwell had sold himself to the devil had begun to circulate during his lifetime. What would be more natural than to tie up a seven year contract with the twin dates of the battle and Cromwell's death? In a bogus letter supposed to have been written by Cromwell, he talks of meeting the devil in human shape and of negotiating a twenty-five year contract. There are many accounts of such alleged meetings and dates are scattered through them. Few of them tie up with genuine historical events. The accounts are a researcher's nightmare.

Cromwell was a man who inspired both intense loyalty and vitriolic hatred not only during his lifetime, but long after his death. While Pettis' references to him must be treated with great caution, they do reflect the fascination the Protector exercised over his countrymen. Even in a small market town like St Ives he was a subject for conjecture, affection and loathing many years after the country had once more become a kingdom.

Chapter 9
John Skeeles

For almost one and a half centuries the Skeeles family were prominent in the commercial life of St Ives. They were carpenters, builders and undertakers. They were also careful observers of what went on in the town, kept private diaries, and have left behind a unique glimpse of life in the town from 1796 to 1930. John Skeeles who died aged about 80 in the 1930s, would certainly have known Norris. No doubt the two men compared notes as they walked the countryside. Perhaps Skeeles even got close to the shy, introverted jeweller. They were both consumed with a passion for local history, the builder from a purely personal point of view, the jeweller dreaming his dreams of writing an important history.

It was John Skeeles who brought order to what must have been a jumble of scribbled family recollections. He produced a journal made up of his own observations, notes left behind by his father, and memories of what his grandfather had told him. This journal was never published, but after his death his journal was typed out and a copy is in the Norris Museum.

Unlike Pettis, Skeeles was not particularly impressed by variations in the climate. He did not record many dramatic freezes or stifling heatwaves. He was, however, interested in the countryside. He lovingly depicts Hemingford Meadows as offering "a pleasing and constant change of colouring. Frost bitten grass turning green and then grey with abundance of daisies early in spring. Then a gorgeous sheet of yellow buttercups followed by various shades of mauve, green and brown before grass cutting starts. Then parched by sun, then flood and ice".

It was on Hemingford Meadow that an attempt was made to make St Ives the scene of a nationally recognised flat race meeting. This little known fact is established by an entry in the Racing Calendar in 1781. For a racecourse to be recognised by the Jockey Club, its races have got to be listed in the Racing Calendar, the bible of the racing world.

In 1781 two Huntingdonshire venues are listed. One is Portholme where important flat race meetings took place at that time. The other is St Ives. There is no explanation for this, and there is no clue as to where the fixture took place. It was probably on Hemingford Meadow. It will surprise most of the residents of St Ives today to learn that the town once staged race meetings with Jockey Club approval. No local records survive and there are no racing exhibits in the Norris Museum.

But the Racing Calendar insists that from 1781 to 1788 an attempt was made to hold an annual summer meeting. Anyone trying to start a new racecourse today faces enormous difficulties, but two hundred years ago the Jockey Club was more paternal in its attitude. Official recognition would have been easier to obtain. Travelling about the country was not easy, and there were plenty of meetings drawing their crowds solely from the surrounding area.

The first fixture was in September 1781 and the chief trophy was the Town Cup. There were three runners in this race. The next day entries were again scarce. From then until 1788 the organisers struggled to keep the fixture going. The last meeting was in September 1788. There were three races spread over two days, and one filly, Creeping Kate, won on both days. This is the last mention of St Ives in the Racing Calendar.

It is ironic to reflect that less than a hundred years later, in November 1885, Huntingdon established a National Hunt racecourse which today is one of the most successful in the country. Top owners and trainers send their horses there, and the country's leading jockeys negotiate the obstacles as they race over Waterloo Meadows.

John Skeeles was also interested in geography. He notes that Dr Arnold of Rugby was fond of saying that looking east from his school, there was nothing between him and the Ural mountains, Holland, North Germany and central Russia being all part of the great European plain. Skeeles adds to this quotation that the fens covered roughly 750,000 acres and were part of this plain. He reflects that the Danes, when they invaded Britain, would frequently have sailed up the Ouse past the spot where St Ives now stands. There was much fighting in the area when the Danes ravaged the country. The invaders suffered a severe defeat by Edward the Elder at Tempsford, and he wrested back possession of Huntingdon from them. Skeeles recalls the story that king Canute had a hunting lodge built at Bodsey, near Ramsey. This is historically questionable.

Like Pettis, Skeeles refers to the great fire of 1689. His account is not as graphic as that of his predecessor, but it does fill in some gaps in Pettis' version. He says that the fire "does not appear to have spread much north of White Hart Lane. On the opposite side of Market Hill, the extreme limit of the fire seems to have been directly opposite the present White Hart public house".

The strong wind appears to have been north easterly. The Robin Hood was damaged and as the fire spread down Bridge Street, it severely damaged all the Elizabethan and Jacobean buildings. These have been demolished one by one since 1800. While the fire lasted, the thatched roofs would have encouraged it to spread rapidly. St Ives would have had a plentiful supply of reeds and straw and roofing tiles were still a comparative novelty. A number of thatched buildings stretching from The Waits almost to West Street were gutted within a few hours in a more recent blaze that Skeeles had witnessed. According to Skeeles, the last three thatched buildings he could recall in the town were a cottage in North Road, a building in East Street and a beer store at the Ramsey Road brewery.

It was John Skeeles' great grandfather, Richard, who erected the clock tower in Bridge Street in 1802 which became such a famous landmark over the years, and is remembered by some residents of St Ives to this day. It was also to prove, 120 years later, a source of embarrassment for the then borough council. An account book which Richard Skeeles handed on to his son shows that in 1802 he was commissioned to build a house and two shops for the Duke of Manchester. The clock tower formed part of this set of buildings, which cost £230.

Skeeles' journal contains several entries for work and materials in connection with fixing the clock. They include the cost of pulleys and casings, and weights. On March 26, April 10, May 17, June 4 and July 16, 1803 the journal lists various charges, and even when the clock tower was erected, there continued to be a stream of running costs. On March 28, 1804, Richard Skeeles notes: "Altering pulleys and casing. A wheel 3/-". On November 9, 1805 there are more charges, and in 1808 he was preoccupied with the clock again. One entry reads: "A two stone weight for clock, rollers for ditto, cutting away girders for weights, altering case etc". The clock tower was included in a dispersal sale of some of the Duke of Manchester's property in July 1918, and was pulled down four years later.

It was when the borough council first turned its attention to the future of the clock tower in 1922, that its members realised they faced a problem. Local newspapers at the time tell the story in some detail. At that time the clock stood above the furniture and removals firm of Kiddles, a branch of a Norwich family, which had moved to St Ives in the 1830s. Edward Kiddle had started the business in 1837 in the name of his son, Robert.

The shop originally dealt in furniture, but at various times it also functioned as an undertaker's. It also did decorating work, and about 100 years ago broke into the removals business, using horse-drawn pantechnicons. In 1957 Robin Kiddle, who is now retired and still lives in Bluntisham, opened a perambulator shop in separate premises. The business was sold in 1986.

When borough councillors began looking into the history of the clock tower, they found themselves confronted with an intriguing legal point. The clock belonged to the council, but it was sited on private property. It was one of the few examples of a clock having been built and maintained from public funds, but architecturally supported by a privately owned building.

By now Kiddles building had been judged to be unsafe and required extensive restoration. This meant the clock had to come down. When the council consulted its lawyers, it transpired that it had a right to maintain a clock over premises on that particular site forever, and to have it supported by any building which replaced the original one. Members could not make up their minds about the clock's future, and it was pointed out to them that if the clock were not replaced when restoration work was over, the council would automatically lose its right to have a clock there in the future.

This appeared to be a simple enough decision to make, but the matter became complicated when Edward Kiddle, then in charge of the family business, began demolition work. He discovered that the clock depended entirely on his roof for support. It had always been thought that the clock's supports went down to the foundation of the walls. Kiddle now declared that he was unable to go ahead with his work until the tower supporting the clock was removed. He also claimed, to the alarm of some council members, that had it not been for the weight of the clock, he would not have had to pull his property down. He argued that in high winds the tower swayed noticeably, and that over the years this movement had pushed his roof over by several inches. Visions of a claim for damages danced before the council's eyes, and there was a good deal of discussion as to what should be done.

Kiddle said he certainly was not going to put on a new roof until something had been done about supporting the tower, so that the clock would no longer depend for its safety upon his roof. It had been threatening his property over the years. The clock had been sheltered from the weather by a picturesque cupola, and when Kiddle, a former mayor, was asked what sort of shelter he planned to provide, he was forthright in his reply: "I think I know what you mean", he told the councillors. "You want to know whether I shall put in a roof as picturesque as the clock to be in keeping with it. I am fond of the clock, but not fond enough to build a picturesque roof to fit it. I am going to put on something which will not cost much money, a modern roof".

The matter was debated at several council meetings with Kiddle agreeing that while the council had a right to place a clock on his roof, he could not be expected to pay for any extra supporting work for cosmetic reasons. Most councillors agreed that the clock was no longer needed by the town. When it was first erected, clocks and watches had been scarce. Now even errand boys wore watches. In addition the post office had a clock, the parish church had one and there was an illuminated one on Market Hill on the spire of the Free Church. There were, however, traditionally minded councillors who argued it would not be right to remove a town landmark. It was finally decided that the clock should come down, and that its future would be debated later.

When the clock was brought down an inscription was discovered on it.
It read: Made by subscription
           John Constable Churchwardens
           John Mann
           John Briant, maker, Hertford 1803.

The building itself on which the clock rested used to belong to the Duke of Manchester and by 1922 had been the home of the Kiddle family for nearly 90 years. In 1918 Edward Kiddle bought it from the duke. It was belived to be almost 400 years old, and was at one time a public house. At the rear of the shop next door, also owned by the Kiddles, a beautiful oak ceiling was discovered during alteration work shortly before the outbreak of the 1914 war.

Apparently when Richard Skeeles built the premises, some existing buildings had been taken down, and the materials had been used again as far as possible. The Elizabethan timbering must have been left intact.

The history of the clock after it was taken down is a sorry tale. Whether the council debated its future or not, is not recorded, but evidently there was never a move to have it re-erected. It was at first taken by lorry to a loft above Fowells engineering works in New Road, and later stored in a shed behind the town hall. In the mid-sixties it was offered to the Norris Museum, but the curator, Mervyn Coote, declined it. Amputated from its stately tower, it was just another clock. To have re-sited it upon a tower in the grounds of the museum would have been expensive, and the clock, which was once a friendly landmark and later a cause for concern, was declared worthless. Robin Kiddle believes it ended its days buried in a municipal rubbish dump in the nearby village of Hemingford Abbots.

Skeeles took a great interest in the development of the town, and his description of conditions in the early nineteenth century makes appalling reading. In writing this section, he says he was drawing upon what his grandfather and his father told him, and also on his own lifetime of recollections stretching over more than 70 years. He also had the experience of 60 years in the building trade.

At the beginning of the century St Ives was an extremely cramped town, wanting to, but not yet able to expand geographically. An increasing population was herded into what were, for the most part, the original streets and the small alleyways and courtyards leading off them. The reason for this congestion was not far to seek. The manorial system of land ownership, with its arbitary charges on changes in ownership, discouraged development. In addition, a good deal of grassland was reserved for cattle, this land being tied up in many cases to various licensed houses who accommodated the drovers who brought their animals to the weekly Monday markets. All this was an obstacle to building.

By the early 1800s there were very few houses on the Hemingford side of the bridge apart from three public houses including the Dolphin. The old Slepe Hall estate virtually cordoned off the east and north east sides of the town, before Oliver Road, The Quadrant, Cromwell Place and Cromwell Terrace existed. East Street was thinly filled in and courtyards sprang up wherever room could be found for them. An ability to cram as many tiny houses as possible into a limited space was a vital qualification for any architect.

One local builder, John Green, had that quality to a high degree. The most congested area lay between the Sheep Market and the river. It was a period during which living conditions were wretched for the majority of the residents who lived crowded, squalid lives. Skeeles writes: "It needs little imagination to picture the insanitary state of the town from 1800 onwards, with increasing population. No wonder that the death rate was high, and that outbreaks of fevers, smallpox and cholera were almost of annual occurrence". Those who died from highly infectious diseases were buried at dead of night. Skeeles refers to a story concerning Bateman Brown, the son of wealthy Houghton miller, Potto Brown. He was out for a stroll one Sunday evening and was told by a boy he met on Market Hill that there would be ten burials that night. The unfortunate victims of cholera or smallpox were interred hastily and without ceremony. A handful of sobbing relatives would follow the coffin as it was hurried furtively to the graveyard. In 1832 a bad epidemic swept through the town causing a great many deaths. Many of the victims of serious infectious diseases are said to have been buried in what came to be known as the "new ground" in the parish churchyard, that is in the corner nearest to the Dun Horse.

This custom of burying corpses in the dark led to bizarre, almost eerie incidents. A member of the Improvement Commissioners, aware that a victim of smallpox was to be buried that night, went down to the graveyard at dusk to see that everything had been prepared. As darkness was falling, he stepped on the planks above the open grave, and was startled to hear a plaintive "baa". It was coming from a sheep which had fallen into the grave and was in danger of being buried with the corpse. It was the custom at the time to let a flock of sheep loose in churchyards to keep the grass short.

The town's only water supply came from the river or from a few wells, most of which were polluted. Skeeles paints a picture of conditions in one row of cottages he knew well as a child. "They were superior", he recalls, "having small backyards. In each yard was a convenience with its cesspool under and in some cases a pigsty too. His Majesty 'Pig' walked through the house to live or die, and the contents of the cesspool and dung pit alike were also carried through. The heat of a July or August day rendered the atmosphere unbearable.

"Scores of houses faced only little narrow yards, frequently with no ventilation at the back . . . one pump and one convenience for a whole row of cottages. Can one wonder that drunkenness, quarrelling and immorality were rife?"

Skeeles frequently witnessed on hot afternoons two enraged women screaming abuse while at the same time struggling to scratch and bite one another, they would come rolling out from one of the yards, carrying their fight to the sheep pens on the market.

The Skeeles were meticulous costers. Some items from their old account books throw light on wages and the costs of building materials in the last century.

1801. Carpenter and joiner 3d per hour. Elouance (allowance) extra.
A man three days elouance 8/6.
Self ¾ day 2.2¼d = 2/11 per day.
Ditto 1¾ days 4.7½d = 2/8 per day.
Son 2/6 per day.
1818. Master 3/6 per day. Apprentice 2/9.
1829. Man 3/6 per day. Boy 1/0 Improver 2/9.
1831. Man 4/0 Boy 2/3 Improver 3/0.

John Skeeles' great grandfather and grandfather were cabinet makers as well as being skilled carpenters and joiners. In 1801 brickwork cost £11.11. per rod and five bushels of lime 18s. Painting work was charged at 7d a yard. In 1806 the company charged £18.4. for reeds for a cottage roof on Houghton Hill.

Skeeles' journal also goes into the cost of food at the end of the eighteenth and beginning of the nineteenth centuries. The cost of food, clothing and house rents were serious items for the average family in years of very low wages. In 1795 a stone of flour cost 3s. Four years later a pint of rum was 1s.9d as was a pint of wine. A breast of mutton cost half a crown, and a leg of beef 1s.6d. In 1800 three stone of beef was 19s.6d, suet cost between eight and ten pence a pound. Two stone of flour cost 11s and a whole cheese 13s. Five and three quarter pounds of beef fetched 4s.1d and a bushel of potatoes, one shilling. Veal was 8d a pound and pork seven. A bushel of apples cost 2s.9d in 1809, but three years later it had gone up to 7s.6d. Honey was 9s.2d. for ten pounds. Even in the cramped conditions in which they lived, many people kept a pig. Two pigs in 1802 cost £2.1s.

One member of the Skeeles family spent £2.5.3d on a shopping expedition which included: one pig 18s. 11 bushels of brewers grain 2s.9d, oats 2s.6d and a bushel of beans 3s. There were also three bushels of barley for 12s and six stone of barley meal for 7s.

With food a vital cost factor for families that tended to be large, it is not surprising that when prices rose sharply, discontent followed. In 1798 the price of food soared because of a poor harvest the previous summer. One Monday morning a group of St Ives housewives stormed through the market inciting others to violence. They seized butter, meat, fruit and vegatables and sold them to each other. They then began booing and hissing the millers and corn dealers, threatening to throw them all in the river. The threatened victims of this summary form of justice wisely retired to the public houses until the authorities succeeded in restoring law and order.

In 1801 the Skeeles household expenditure on furniture is listed: A bed £3. A pair of blankets 13s.6d. Two bureaus, one costing £2.16. and the other £3.10. A flock bed £1.2.3d and sampler frames 4s.3d. Rents at the time on small houses and cottages were between £4 and £10 a year.

That was the year when a bullock caused pandemonium in the town on a January market day. It wandered into the passage beside the Royal Oak in Crown Street and, finding a door open, went upstairs and walked into the dining room which fortunately was empty at the time. After a while the animal got restive and tried to get out. Seeing the ground below, it charged through a window, driving the glass and the entire window frame into the street. The bullock followed this cascade and, though uninjured, was by now terrified. It bolted in the direction of the bridge. Terrified shoppers ran in all directions as the bullock galloped down Bridge Street. It was finally headed off at the bridge where it was cornered. It leapt into the river which was swollen by flood, and the strong tide carried the animal downstream to its death.

Being an undertaker, Skeeles knew all about funeral customs, and devotes a section of his memoirs to them. An act passed in 1666 which was tightened 12 years later, had laid down that shrouds must be made of wool, and that coffins should be lined with the same material. The idea had been to encourage the wool trade, but the acts gradually fell into disuse, and had been repealed by the time Skeeles became an undertaker. When he started in business, coffins were generally lined with flannel.

He recalls the days when undertakers had to pay their visits to bereaved relatives stealthily by night, and when funerals were deferred one week "to show proper respect". During those seven days the open coffin containing the corpse would lie in the house of the nearest relative so that family, friends and other mourners could gaze respectfully for the last time on the features of the dead person.

Another reason for delaying a burial in some cases was to allow funerals to take place on a Sunday when, presumably, it would have been easier for mourners to attend. Skeeles deplores this practice, and talks of bodies often becoming "offensive to everyone in the house". He also talks of a coffin being regarded as "a bogey, or object of terror", particularly where children were concerned.

In St Ives this custom of delaying funerals for a Sunday burial was radically changed when the Rev. Charles Goldie became vicar of All Saints. This bustling cleric swept into the parish, promptly sacked the incumbent curate and introduced his brand of no-nonsense, practical religion to a slightly bewildered community. He lost no time in consulting with the nonconformist ministers and convinced the people there was no real need for a prolonged period of "showing respect".

In 1801 orders were issued that coffins had to be used to bury the bodies of paupers. Previously people on very small incomes were lowered into their graves wrapped only in a shroud. The new orders laid down strict limits on the amount of money that could be spent. Money would only be provided for the simplest coffins with no lining, though kindly undertakers would risk a penalty by providing a very plain one. Initial letters or a cheap brass plate were ruled out. Sometimes the order to the undertaker would specify two yards of calico for a shroud, but frequently the naked corpses of the dead, their hands and feet secured with string, were lowered into the coffin. There was scarcely any end to the distress of relatives of the poor at their time of bereavement. The undertaker would receive an order with the amount to be spent precisely stated. The order would also contain a warning that if the specified amount were exceeded "the extra will not be paid".

This practice of naked burial raised strong feelings everywhere, and finally the Guardians of the Poor agreed that at even the poorest of burials a worn out shirt or nightdress might be used to clothe the body. The situation only really improved with the advent and spread of industrial life assurance policies. These policies, for which people paid minute sums annually to provide for a decent funeral, were enthusiastically sold by agents, leading to jibes about "death hunters".

The funerals of the well-off, on the other hand, were spectacular affairs and were indeed black. Skeeles writing about some he organised writes: "In those days a hearse was a black box on wheels surmounted by groups of black ostrich plumes. The black horses also had black cloths and black plumes on their heads. The undertakers, drivers, assistants and mourners were all in black with silk hats or crepe hat bands, black scarves etc. The pervading blackness has always been clearly printed on my memory."

There were no wheeled hand biers in Skeeles' time. The coffin would be borne by up to a dozen men whose subsequent expense accounts for refreshments could be startling. These expenses were in addition to the fees they charged for doing the job. Among his papers Skeeles had a record of the fact that the landland of the Cow and Hare was paid £2.9s.2d for drink at one funeral in 1853. In that year a substantial amount of ale could be drunk for that sum.

One of Skeeles' hobbies was to trace family names that had survived for centuries and he made a particular study of old St Ivian names. In 1930 he wrote down a list of 311 well known family names during his lifetime and that of his father and grandfather. He discovered that 229 of them had died out. When he was working, Osborne was one of the longest surviving names, the family having been associated with business in the town since 1808. Ulph and Whaley were two other venerable names, and Skeeles believed that the Barton who lived in Bridge Street in 1930, was the fourth or fifth successive holder of that family name. Coote was another name Skeeles listed, together with Edwards, Meadows and Bryant. He also mentions Waldock, Meadows the carpenter, the Ashton family of millers and the solicitors Allpress. In 1806 the Ansley family were large property owners both in St Ives and Houghton.

Under the heading "unusual names" the builder records: Bullbrooke, Brumage, and Boyer. The Barnes family gave their name to Barnes Walk, and the Blooms owned the White Horse Hotel near the Dolphin. Skeeles could remember two Bloom brothers and a sister who was a milliner in Crown Street. After one brother died, the surviving one had a house built in London Road with a view to using it as a retirement home. Unfortunately he died in it the night after he moved in.

Skeeles also writes at length about the chapel on the bridge. This, the most photographed and probably the most publicised landmark of St Ives, is mentioned by all three of the chroniclers who lived in St Ives. Its story has been told and re-told, the latest author to have researched its history being Bob Burn-Murdoch, the curator of the Norris Museum, whose book, *St Ives Bridge and Chapel*, was published last year.

The bridge was dedicated to St Leger in 1426, the ceremony probably marking the completion of the present stone bridge, built by the monks of Ramsey Abbey to attract pilgrims to St Ivo's shrine and to make the town more accessible for the traders and merchants coming to the town's international fair.

The last prior of St Ivo's priory was allowed to retire to the chapel to live out the rest of his life after the Dissolution of the monasteries in 1539. It would have provided a tranquil retirement house with spectacular views both up and down the Ouse for a religious man who, for the last years of his life had only his memories of the great monastic tradition to occupy his thoughts.

In 1736 it underwent extensive restoration work. The most dramatic change it underwent was to have two additional storeys built. By all accounts this did nothing to improve the appearance of the chapel. It became unsightly. Reading contemporary descriptions of it, one gets the impression it looked rather like a dumpy dowager poised on the edge of the bridge about to topple into the river.

While it remained a four-storey structure for the next 200 years, it passed through many hands. For a time it was used as a private house, and at least one housewife is known to have strung her washing out on the roof of the building. The tenants would have had superb views both up and down the river, but the arrival of motor cars and lorries imparted a sense of danger to the occupants.

Fig. 13. St Ives bridge and chapel (*above*), showing the extra two storeys on top of the chapel; and a fenland lighter in the Old River behind Wellington Street.

For a brief period it became a public house, and a very unsavoury one at that. In the cramped space where once people worshipped, enormous amounts of beer were drunk, and drunken fights erupted. In an age when people were generally broad minded, the pub's reputation became so bad that it was known locally as "Little Hell".

That prim historian, Norris, was so appalled by what he heard, that he could not bring himself to mention the pub's soubriquet. No doubt pursing his lips as he wrote, he records: "The public house on the bridge was a notoriously bad one and was popularly called by a name we shall not repeat. Pigs were kept in the cellar. During a drunken brawl on a fair-day, a man was thrown over the balcony into the river and was almost drowned". Another writer tells of a baker named "Bustle" Wood who, filled with Dutch courage, took on a bet he could swim from the bridge to the Staunch, a distance of about a quarter of a mile. The river was in full flood, but Wood leapt into it. The cold water obviously sobered him up sharply, and he realised he was in danger of drowning. Fortunately he was pulled out a short distance downstream.

In the spring of 1928 the chapel was bought by George Day, the Town Clerk, and veteran borough councillor Frederic Warren. They presented it to the town, and it was taken over by Huntingdonshire County Council. The chapel had by now been scheduled as an Ancient Monument, and it was evident that the two upper storeys were proving too much for the foundations.

After a report from the Society for the Preservation of Ancient Buildings, it was decided to restore the building and return it to its original size. The county council agreed to meet £150 of the £400 the work would cost, and a public appeal was made for the balance. By April 1930 the restoration work was completed.

The bridge and its chapel remained in the hands of the Huntingdonshire County Council until the local government reorganisation of 1974 did away with the old county of Huntingdonshire. Responsibility for both the bridge and chapel then passed to the Transport Department of Cambridgeshire County Council. Until 1980 fleets of buses and lorries continued to rumble over the bridge, making life for pedestrians hazardous, but in that year St Ives bypass was opened, and traffic over the bridge was dramatically reduced.

The chapel is still used from time to time for religious services, but is now basically a tourist attraction. Keys to it are available at several places in the town. In the summer children hurl themselves into the river from its roof, and from the outside the tiny chapel looks much as it must have done when the last prior of St Ivo's priory went to live in it in 1539. In what is now a modern, busy market town, the chapel exudes a slightly mediaeval air as if still whispering the last enchantements of the fifteenth century.

Skeeles talks about a number of trades and industries he saw in the town during his lifetime which were extinct by 1930. They included brickmaking, lime burning, the barge industry, brewing and malting, candle and pipemaking, rushworking and milling.

Because of the abundance of rushes in the river, rushworking thrived for most of the nineteenth century. The rushes were cut, dried and used for making chair seats, hassocks and kneeler mats. Coopers also used them for fashioning water-tight joints for their vats and coolers.

A candle making business was carried on in premises in East Street, but was closed down in the 1850s. Skeeles writes: "Friday night was the usual time for rendering down the accumulated fat of the week obtained from the butchers. In hot weather on Friday nights and Saturday mornings the smell was appalling. In spite of this it was called a 'healthy' trade, and certainly all the men I can remember being connected with the trade, lived to an advanced age". The factory did not rely for its supplies of fat entirely on local butchers, but also used to import Russian tallow in hogsheads each weighing up to a ton.

When Skeeles was a boy, there were many prosperous barge owners in the town, as before the advent of the railway, the river was an important waterway for transporting goods.

The Bridge Pool was at times so congested, an active person could cross the river by leaping from barge to barge. Horses were used for towing and sail was not unknown. In the 1860s one company caused a sensation by buying a paddle steamer. "As a boy I frequently watched it fussing about with the barges near the mill, and sometimes towing a string of them up to Houghton or Godmanchester", Skeeles notes.

Celebrations organised in 1809 to mark the start of George III's golden jubilee year were extensively reported in the *Cambridge Chronicle* and also in a quaintly worded pamphlet. The unnamed author of this leaflet appears to have been both an ardent royalist and a devout christian, for he reports the full text of the sermon preached in the parish church by the vicar, the Rev. Cuthbert Johnson Baines.

The vicar had taken as his text the 21st verse from the 24th chapter of Proverbs: "My son, fear thou the Lord and the King and meddle not with them that are given to change". How this text went down in St Ives, a town traditionally known for its tendency towards nonconformity and anti-royalist sentiments, is not recorded.

According to the less sycophantic Cambridge newspaper, the morning was ushered in with the firing of cannon and the ringing of church bells. After this, virtually the entire town assembled on Market Hill where a curious form of class distinction prevailed. The *Chronicle* reported that the crowd was mustered in groups. There were the civic dignitaries and officials taking an active part in the pageantry. There were the schoolchildren together with their teachers. Then, standing together on one side of the market, there were "the poor men, women and children of the town", who, presumably had undergone some form of means test before being allocated their humble role.

The vicar commanded the most attentive silence while he spoke, and after the church service the procession marched back to the market, headed by a military band playing *God Save the King* and *Rule Britannia* alternately. After parading the centre of the town, the band drew up outside the Crown Inn where they delivered their colours before dispersing.

The townspeople also broke ranks, with the poor, who numbered more than 1,000 out of a population of less than 4,000, in high spirits as they knew that a feast of meat, bread and beer had been organised for them. Most of the wealthy residents ate at the Crown Inn.

Drinking was a favourite form of relaxation during the nineteenth century and indeed, there are indications of a creeping form of alcoholism. In September 1855, an anonymous correspondent, signing himself "a teacher", wrote to a local newspaper, bewailing the scenes of drunkenness that apparently marked the town's celebrations at the fall of Sebastopol.

"If you sir", he wrote to the editor, "had been an eye witness to the shocking scenes of daily and nightly occurrence here last week, your spirit would have been stirred within you, and you would have imagined the whole town given up to drunkenness . . . you will scarcely believe, sir, that men – fathers – were found to give intoxicating drinks to children not their own, to boys and girls of tender age until they could drink no more, became incapable of taking care of themselves, and had to be carried away from the disgusting scene in a state of helpless intoxication. And this too, in St Ives, in the second half of the nineteenth century".

Penalities for public drunkenness handed out in those days would amaze today's magistrates whose powers are now curtailed. At the Petty Sessions on February 15, 1875, labourer Thomas Goodjohn was charged with being drunk and riotous while in receipt of parish money. This was the equivalent of today's dole, but then was only given in desperate cases. Goodjohn was sentenced to six weeks hard labour.

Life was a rough and tumble affair in the nineteenth century. It was a rumbustious age which saw the growth of the industrial revolution, and significant changes in rural life. These changes, by and large, passed St Ives by making scarely a mark on the fabric of the town's society. The century did throw up men of great business acumen such as Potto Brown of Houghton. It was also an age which produced men with strong social consciences. The Day family provided successive town clerks for the borough council, and the Groves ministered to the town's medical needs. It had its characters such as "Bustle" Wood, not to mention its derelicts like Thomas Goodjohn.

People worked hard and, at times of national rejoicing feasted and drank hard. The nineteenth century was not a time for feebleness. It was an enquiring, thrusting era which witnessed technological advances on a wide front. St Ives, with its thriving Monday market, its mediaeval chapel, its memories of St Ivo and the golden days of the international trade fair, entered the twentieth century with confidence. One can almost see Norris prowling the town in search of historical knowledge, and Skeeles bent over his father's accounts books leaving for posterity a mirror reflecting the life of a town at the dawn of a new age.

Chapter 10
Political Passions

Political life in England in the nineteenth century was marked by passion. Speakers tended to make flowery speeches, and also very long ones. Political meetings before the arrival of first the radio and then of television drew enormous crowds and speakers felt they deserved to be entertained. The rhetoric deployed during modern election campaigns is pallid compared with the ferocity bordering on hysteria with which speakers addressed their audiences a century ago.

Writs flew as personal insults were cheerfully exchanged. Reputations were frequently impugned and crowds often turned ugly if they disagreed with what they were being told. It was a common occurrence for fights to break out and it was commonplace for people to be maimed or even killed. Elderly speakers, many of them replete with good food and stimulated with port, drove themselves to near apoplexy and it was not unheard of for candidates with suspect health, with weight problems or with dangerous blood pressure levels, to collapse in front of their listeners.

St Ives was no exception to the general rule, and committed Conservative and Liberal candidates threw themselves at the hustings with an enthusiasm frequently laced with malice, calumny and libel. Britain's foreign secretary, John Major, whose parliamentary constituency embraces St Ives, is unlikely to consider issuing writs against any of his rivals during a general election. A hundred years ago the possibility would have been very much on his mind.

We have seen how Henry Cromwell, or Williams as he called himself by 1673, died when a candidate nominated by him lost a closely fought election in Huntingdon. The historian Mark Noble gives a detailed account of the campaign which led to Williams' death on a stifling August day in 1673.

Lionel Walden, one of Huntingdon's MPs, had died during a parliamentary session and Charles II approached Williams, who was also an MP and enquired: "Well, Williams, who shall we have now for your borough?" Williams, an influential man in the county, arrogantly replied: "It shall be whom I think proper."

The monarch, who enjoyed making mischief, retailed this conversation to the Earl of Manchester who took up the challenge remarking: "I will let Williams know it shall not be whom he thinks proper." He then nominated a candidate of his own and a particularly bruising campaign was launched. When the closely run contest was over and Williams heard his man had lost, he collapsed in the chair in which he was sitting in a Huntingdon hotel and died.

We do not know which tavern this lethal drinking spree took place in but certainly vast amounts of alcohol were consumed by everyone involved in an election campaign. By an ironic twist of fate, Williams' seat in Parliament was in turn filled by Rob Apreece of Washingley, his nominee and defeated candidate for Walden's seat.

In those days people interested in politics could expect free hospitality from candidates providing they voted for the man whose money they were taking. There was no possibility of accepting food and drink from more than one candidate. The secret ballot had not yet arrived, and on voting day each voter mounted a rostrum in the county town when his name was called and clearly announced for whom he was voting. Anyone who had dined and drunk at one candidate's expense before the poll and then went and voted for someone else, would have been foolhardy in the extreme.

The amount of money candidates spent on hospitality was extraordinary. In his book *British and Irish Elections 1794–1831*, Peter Jupp gives a breakdown of the election expenses of Lord Mandeville and William Fellowes for an election in Huntingdonshire in 1826. The total amount was £13,384, with each candidate paying half – there were two seats for the county. After some quaint items such as £65.14.6d. for "ringers in several towns," and £38.13.0d. for drums and fifes, comes the biggest single item. It is for "innkeepers' bills thro' the county," and amounts to £6,834.11.3d, more than half the expenses. Music cost the two candidates £143.15.0d. while counsel, no doubt standing by ready to repel any charges of libel, submitted fees for £723.10.0d.

A typical political *cause célèbre* involving St Ives took place during the 1830s. George Game Day was a respected solicitor who was also a convinced Liberal and he often did political work for that party free of charge. The right to vote was confined to those whose names appeared on the official voters register. To be registered a man had to fulfil certain conditions regarding income or property, and agents for both major parties worked tirelessly to add the names of their respective supporters to this roll.

George Day, with his knowledge of the law, was active in this work, and in 1835 succeeded in getting 320 new voters registered and 187 Tory claimants rejected. The Conservatives countered by bringing to light what they described as a piece of Liberal sharp practice. It appeared Day had arranged for the Liberals to buy a large plot of unused land at Hartford, this was then divided up among 43 separate owners, and it was claimed they fulfilled the conditions relating to property. Day was forced to concede that some of these owners did not in fact fulfil the conditions, and they were thrown off the register. However, the persistent lawyer got them back on the following year.

This occurred between elections, and both parties continued sparring, with Day being far more successful than his opposite number in the Conservative party. He was challenged at every turn, on the validity of dates, on conveyancing documents, on whether stamps on documents were purchased outside the constituency limits – in those days stamps were marked with the name of the post office selling them – and on the alleged secrecy of his political dealings.

Finally, the frustrated Tories brought him before the Assizes, with Day complaining he had only been informed this was going to happen at the last moment, and that he had been unable to see the actual charge until minutes before the case came before the court. In the event the court ruled in his favour and all the charges were dismissed.

The case caused a local sensation, as the air had been thick with accusations and counter allegations. A vindicated Day returned to his practice, but not before he had received effusive tributes, publicly paid by leading Liberals.

On January 25th, 1837, he was the guest of honour at a lavish banquet held in the Priory Barn at which he was presented with magnificent silver plate worth 1,000 guineas. Earl Fitzwilliam was the chairman at the dinner which was attended by just about every Liberal of note in the area, and the guest list read like a Who's Who of county society.

Contemporary accounts of this banquet, as well as the opening speeches which were published verbatim in book form and priced at a shilling, make fascinating reading and also illustrate how, in an age before the arrival of radio and television, public speaking was raised almost to an art form.

The stylistic prose of the reporter, and the rounded, florid sentences of the after dinner speakers, some of whom displayed a tendency to raid the classics, are far removed from the punchy style of modern journalists and the less declamatory tone of modern election candidates, both of whom are far more restrained today by the laws of libel.

A Mr Weston Hatfield took it upon himself to preserve for posterity the events of the Priory Barn banquet in his book entitled somewhat laboriously *Presentation of One Thousand Guineas in Plate to George Game Day Esq*. He records: "The tables were exceedingly well served on handsome blue ware. The viands were excellent, consisting of soup, poultry, tongues, hams etc in addition to the more substantial old English fare of roast beef and plum pudding, confectionery etc. The wines were excellent." Mr Hatfield concludes with a nod towards the providers of this feast: "The whole reflecting great credit upon the worthy host and hostess of the Crown Hotel."

After introductory speeches Day chose to go in great detail through the events that had led to his indictment and acquittal. His speech is a fine example of an after dinner speaker 150 years ago. According to the attentive Hatfield, Day was constantly interrupted with loud "hear hears." There was frequent prolonged cheering and, during the sarcastic bits, much laughter.

Day reached back into history when he declared: "It is reported, my Lord, to have been a saying of the ancient Goths, 'when we want to brand an enemy with infamy, we call him a Roman' thereby meaning all that is base and dishonourable. When the modern Goths, my Lord, desire to brand an enemy with infamy, they call him a 'Radical'. With the Goths I am a Roman, with the Tories I am a Radical."

Day went on to ride the wind. He spoke of "Tory malignant falsehoods and misrepresentations of facts." He claimed that his opponents, in an attempt to wreck his professional reputation, had publicly stated he was about to be fined, imprisoned and perhaps even transported. It was a bravura performance. No modern politician would get away with it.

Day also claimed he had been unable to identify his accuser before the case was heard. "I applied to the conductors of the prosecution," he cried. "I applied to the court. In every case I was told that himself and his dagger were concealed. In vain did I urge that true soldiers fought under colours fully displayed. In vain did I protest against this Spanish peasant mode of concealed musket warfare. Instead of a manly opponent, I had a secret assassin." It must have been a riveting evening.

Chapter 11
An Illustrious Market

If a commercial directory had been published in 1893 of the trades and industries which flourished in St Ives at the time, it would have included one firm of auctioneers, three architects and surveyors and one aerated water manufacturer. It would have listed seven builders and carpenters, nine boot and shoe makers and four brewers. It would have gone on to give details of four blacksmiths, six butchers, nine bakers and two basket makers.

The directory would have been incomplete if it had not included three bankers, three carriage builders, two chemists and five coal merchants. Three confectioners, two corn merchants and six cattle dealers would have made sure they were not left out, and their names would have appeared alongside those of two fellmongers, six greengrocers and florists, and seven fancy goods stores.

The town had only a single fishmonger, but there were four furniture dealers and upholsterers, 12 grocers and two gas and water fitters. Four hairdressers catered for the latest trend in hair styles, and there were three milliners. Three doctors looked after the town's health while one piano and organ tuner served the musical. There were five ironmongers, two newspapers and two photographers, while on the heavier side there were six painters and plumbers and two saddle and harness makers. There were eight tailors, drapers and outfitters, four printers and booksellers and five solicitors. Four jewellers looked after the town's decorative requirements and parents had the choice of nine schools for their children. The resident population at the time was about 3000.

These lists of traders were compiled by S. G. Jarman for a pamphlet on the trades and industries of St Ives that he wrote in 1893. But even his impressive figures only tell half the story, for they refer to the resident businesses in St Ives. These were added to every Monday morning by the excitement and bustle of the weekly market.

During the nineteenth century the importance of the weekly Monday markets reached their zenith, though by the turn of the century a marked decline had set in. The market was established by a charter granted by King John in about 1200, and in the mid 1800s it was said to be second only to that held at Smithfield in size and importance. When it first began, one of the main commodities traded was woad with which ancient Britons once dyed themselves.

It then became noted for old clothes and eels, before it emerged as a substantial cattle, sheep and horse market. Thomas Carlisle wrote of St Ives: "A most ancient market on the shores of the sable Ouse". After a new market was built in 1886, a local newspaper declared: "St Ives now possesses one of the most compact, one of the best appointed, one of the best built markets in England. It is fashioned after Leicester, but, excellent as Leicester is, this is marked by later improvements".

In his thesis, *The Marketing of Livestock in St Ives and the Surrounding Area 1830–1900*, Robert Flack, a teacher at Westfield School, gives a good account of how the market worked in the last century. I have based much of this chapter on his researches.

During that period much of the transport network in Britain underwent major changes, the most significant being the coming of the railways. Huntingdonshire had already been both of local and national importance. Its market and fairs had hauled it out of obscurity in the Middle Ages. Goods traded in its towns covered a wide range of agricultural produce, and livestock was a very important matter for St Ives. The town was the end of the line, so to speak, for drovers bringing down lean cattle from Scotland, Ireland, the north and sometimes from Wales. These cattle were grazed in the pastures of Huntingdonshire and so fatstock sales in St Ives gave the town outstanding links outside the county.

Before the arrival of the railways, the main method of moving sheep and cattle around the country was quite literally "on the hoof". The Great North Road was one of the major routes for animals from the north and Scotland, and as late as 1861 the national census discloses that there was a resident bullock shoer in St Ives, indicating that the town was recognised as a halting pace for drovers. The average size of a drove varied between 100 and 400 animals attended by four to eight drovers and their dogs. The animals were driven along in a leisurely fashion in the interests of fitness, grazing along the way.

Transportation could take weeks, so overnight accommodation had to be found for both men and beasts. At St Ives there was plenty of room for the drovers in the pubs and the animals could be placed in adjoining paddocks and surrounding fields (lairage). As St Ives market was on a Monday, drovers customarily arrived at the weekend. Census figures for the mid-nineteenth century show as many as 15 drovers could be lodged in St Ives on a Sunday night.

The railways came at the county from three directions. Between 1846 and 1850 the main north-south link from London, passing through Huntingdon, was built. During the same period Huntingdon was linked to St Ives and from there on to Cambridge and the fens. Finally, between 1875 and 1889, minor local extensions were built. There was no coherent national plan, and so instead of an efficient system linking rural and national lines, the system inside counties was constructed piecemeal.

The Scottish cattle trade upon which St Ives had relied for centuries for cattle to graze, had first been affected when the steamship trade was developed in the 1820s. Railways put paid to the age of the drover, as Scottish meat could go directly to London. Soon it was realised it was not necessary to send live animals, and a dead meat trade, centred on Aberdeen was established.

But the railways and steamships opened up the town to the Irish cattle market and by the early 1860s large supplies were coming to the town's market. This was so marked that, particularly on Fair days (Whitsun and Michaelmas), the bullock market was unable to cope with the number of animals from across the Irish Sea and it overspilled the market limits and extended as far as Green End. Bristol was the major port for the entry of cattle destined for St Ives, but other ports, including Liverpool, also sent cattle.

Irish stock sometimes arrived in poor condition because of the dreadful overcrowding on ships and railways, and constant complaints from local farmers used to appear in the correspondence columns of local newspapers. The railways also had an effect on sheep trading when, in mid-century they opened up arable farms in the east to the remote areas where they were marketed.

Though the long distance drover was gradually made redundant as communications improved, his local counterpart remained a conspicuous figure in rural life. A Bill Freeman, a long standing resident of St Ives, who died in 1962, was a drover at the turn of the century. He could recall taking cattle to Ely and doing the journey of 18 miles in a day. A longer journey involved herding sheep from Kings Lynn to St Ives, a distance of 46 miles. The drover would make overnight stops at Wisbech and Chatteris. Drovers also worked on shorter journeys in the district and the animals still had to be walked from railway stations to the markets. Hume Anderson, a pig dealer who started trading at the end of the century, would employ up to six drovers for taking pigs from the market to the station for loading up for London.

Before the advent of the railways, the journey to the capital took up to a fortnight and it was estimated the value of animals diminished on average three guineas through loss of weight and condition. During this period St Ives market functioned chiefly as a collecting centre for livestock sold to butchers and dealers who forwarded them to towns and cities where they would be slaughtered.

Before the 1860s, imported meat was a very small percentage of the trade in Britain, and what there was came mainly from continental countries. But developments such as canning and especially mechanical refrigeration and chilling techniques in the 1870s, solved the problem of preserving meat during long journeys. This led to the import of meat from the United States, Latin America, Australia and New Zealand, all of whom had surplus livestock.

By 1900 these imports were considerable and they were undercutting home production. Meat prices slumped and St Ives felt the effect. Local newspapers reflected this. The agriculture columnist of the *Hunts County Guardian*, whose pseudonym was "Agricola of the Field", often devoted his column to the subject. Early in 1888 he complained that imports of mutton and beef were damaging local graziers. The correspondence columns were filled with sorrowful letters from farmers.

The resentment was voiced by MPs and Captain Fellowes, member for South Huntingdonshire made a stirring speech at St Ives Market in October 1886. He declared: "We have good railway communications, we have the fame and honour of a good name and of popularity attaching to us and, with these advantages and a determined spirit, no new market will be able to sweep us off the face of the earth."

Good, rousing stuff it may have been, but unfortunately the Captain's confidence was misplaced. St Ives Borough Council had made a more realistic appraisal three years earlier when it minuted it was of the opinion "that the continued importation of cattle from these foreign countries . . . is an injustice to the agriculture of this country".

Only spasmodic and in some cases dubious records of fatstock sales were kept at the time, so it is hard to tell how exactly prices in St Ives suffered, but it is clear they fell sharply.

The influx of foreign meat into Britain coincided, not surprisingly, with outbreaks of diseases which were to devastate home supplies. Many of these diseases had occurred from time to time in Britain, but the free movement of stock between countries increased the hazards, and Britain experienced outbreaks of rinderpest or cattle plague, pleuro-pneumonia and foot and mouth after the controls on the import of meat were lifted.

Foot and mouth first appeared in England in 1839, and over the next 50 years was responsible for greater losses of cattle than all other diseases combined. Pleuro-pneumonia had been diagnosed in England for the first time in 1841, and was particularly virulent in 1865 and 1866 when it coincided with outbreaks of rinderpest. This disease had been active in killing large numbers of cattle in Europe, but was not considered a threat on this side of the channel. One eminent veterinary authority assured the public that "no fear need be entertained that this destructive pest will reach our shores". This optimistic prognosis was uttered in 1857. Eight years later the same authority diagnosed cases of rinderpest in London. Within months the disease was rife.

Huntingdonshire, a reception area for large numbers of cattle, mainly from Ireland, was prone to outbreaks of all three diseases. As a railway junction, cattle not destined for the town passed through and were transferred to other trucks. Between the summer of 1865 and spring of 1866, 1,789 cattle died, and 467 were put down. To this must be added animals infected but slaughtered before they died. The loss to St Ives was great. The whole town was affected as the market was a major revenue raiser. In the crowded, insanitary streets, the town would have been a fertile breeding ground with diseases being transmitted to animals which arrived healthy.

Sheep were also the victims of some of the same diseases and in addition in the mid nineteenth century they were prey to liver rot and sheep pox, the latter being imported along with animals from the continent. In the 1870s these two diseases reduced the number of sheep in the country by ten per cent. No records are available for the town's sheep market during that period, but it is inconceivable that St Ives would have escaped outbreaks of a disease which was having a nationwide effect.

Records are available about outbreaks of swine fever during the latter part of the nineteenth century. This disease reached such proportions by 1878, that it was added to the list of contagious diseases, and in 1893 the Swine Fever Act was passed, giving the Board of Agriculture powers to eliminate it.

St Ives market was severely disrupted by swine fever. From 1886 onwards constant outbreaks were notified and the market was closed in July 1894 and also for considerable periods between December 1896 and May 1898. The closure of the pig market caused much concern and throughout 1897 and 1898, the council kept lobbying the Board of Agriculture, its local MP and the county council to get closures lifted. These appeals were invariably unsuccessful and indeed on one occasion almost had a mortal effect. A Board inspector sent up to adjudicate on yet another appeal, surveyed with distaste the insanitary conditions of the market in general, and threatened to close it down for good.

When the nineteenth century dawned St Ives weekly cattle markets were considered only second to those held at Smithfield, while its sheep, pig and horse markets were also substantial. Cattle and horse sales also played a large role at the fairs. But as the century progressed, the fairs dwindled because of the advent of retail traders which was one result of improving communications and also because of the growth of mass markets. As a result the Whitsun and Michaelmas Fairs survived largely due to livestock sales. The weekly cattle markets were so well known that Huntingdon never really developed as a large trading centre due to competition from "its formidable rival". It remained mainly a political and administrative centre.

The Bullock Market, now the Broadway, had been operating for hundreds of years in the same spot, but the influx of imported cattle in the early 1860s was so great that a much larger area was needed. In the 1870s it was commonplace for as many as 12,000 head of Irish cattle to be shown on a single market day, and the appalling conditions underfoot which the *Hunts County Guardian* regularly drew attention to, must have been in existence week in and week out for years. Trying to cross the street meant taking one's life in one's hands, and attempting to walk down either side of the market, crammed with animals, was a nauseating experience. There were no sanitary facilities for the beasts. Newspapers described roads leading to the market as "crowded with beasts unable to get in to the bullock market until afternoon". Traders spent much of the day preventing cattle from breaking shop windows and the smell must have been intolerable.

During the last quarter of the century the market began to decline mainly due to the effects of disease, government legislation and increasing quantities of imported meat. Prior to this decline an unofficial market had been quietly functioning across the bridge on the south side of the Ouse. Irish dealers in particular tended to trade some of their animals without actually entering the town. This had passed unnoticed when the market had been crammed to capacity, but it became noticeable once trade started to decline. In July 1869 no beasts at all were shown between the Unicorn Inn and the parish church, the heart of the cattle market. The loss from non payment of tolls by those who traded south of the river was now intolerable, and the Duke of Manchester, the market's owner, took a Suffolk dealer to court. The dealer lost his right to sell his cattle unless he entered the town and paid his tolls on the bridge. Market tolls were probably paid at the building on the corner of Market Hill and Priory Road, now a thriving bookmakers.

The market, meanwhile, was acquiring an invidious reputation because of the insanitary conditions in Bullock Market. In 1868 an official complaint was received from the Improvement Commissioners for the town, and two years later the first suggestion was made for building a new market near the station, so clearing the centre of the town of cattle. The matter was discussed and considered too expensive, but the idea resurfaced five years later

Fig. 14. The Broadway (*above*), showing the railings that protected pedestrians when it was used as a cattle market; and Bridge Street, with the old clock tower visible at the far end of the right-hand side.

and the new borough council approached the Duke of Manchester with a view to purchasing the market tolls. This was a leisurely period in local government, and a year later the duke came back with an offer which the councillors felt was excessive. They did, however, record that "the possession of the market tolls would benefit the town if they could be obtained on mutually remunerative terms".

In 1881 a waspish leader in the *Hunts County Guardian* declared that the market was "an eyesore to the reformer, and a stain upon the civic reputation of the town". Apparently stung by this candour, the council once more pondered the idea of ridding itself of this eyesore and in 1882 the duke suggested that the council should pay him £6,000. Not all the town's councillors were prepared to pay this amount to remove the stain on their reputation, but after much debate the pro-marketeers won the day, and the duke's offer was accepted. The noble lord then retracted it. It was two years later that a sale was finally agreed.

By 1883, so bad had become the market's reputation for filthiness that no less an august body than the Privy Council sent a veterinary surgeon to make an inspection. In addition to this menacing development, a new cattle market was opened in Cambridge, and councillors as well as those who made a living by agriculture, might well have felt that St Ives market would be lost forever.

Two sites were considered. One was known as Piggots at the eastern end of the Sheep Market near the White Hart. This was rather a small area and would have precluded any expansion. The second was near the railway station and allowed for expansion. This was the site selected, and building began in the spring of 1886.

The new market opened on October 4th, 1886 and was described by Norris as the best appointed in England. It covered about four acres and there was accommodation for 100 fat bullocks, 2,500 store beasts, 600 fat sheep and 3,000 sheep and lambs. The pig market, privately owned by Dilley and Son, had also been improved. All the market roads and avenues were paved with granite and the pens with blue bricks. There was also an ample water supply for both cleaning and drinking. The market's move allowed the opening of more shops on the renamed Broadway, hitherto a commercial site viewed with some suspicion by many retailers. A few people, such as those who had hired out tying posts or had supplied straw and hay, lost out, and some individuals received compensation. The majority of the town's residents heaved a collective sigh of relief.

Trade had slowly begun to pick up shortly before the new market was built, and its arrival gave this a boost. Indeed on the opening day the new accommodation proved to be inadequate and overflow space had to be used. Over the next three or four years things thrived. Dealers came from Norfolk, Suffolk, Essex, Kent, Bedfordshire and Leicestershire. They even came from as far away as Manchester, York and Nottingham. Even Cambridge dealers who had their own Monday market were to be seen from time to time in St Ives.

The boom flattered only to deceive. By 1891 a decline had once more set in and, though there were going to be brief periods of growth in subsequent years, the overall pattern was gloomy. Dealers often could not fill a pen, and were loth to share one. The overflow market became used less and less and ended up as a playground.

One reason for this was the proximity of the new Cambridge market. Only a dozen miles apart and linked by rail, the two markets were inevitably thrown into rivalry. While the Bullock Market was still the shambles it had been before 1886, the better facilities at Cambridge had enticed away nearly all the Irish dealers. Some of them returned when the new St Ives market was opened, but by the early 1890s the Irish had virtually abandoned the small town for the university one.

The loss of the Irish trade was a massive blow. It was never regained. This can be seen in newspaper reports at the turn of the century when the appearance of Irish cattle in St Ives was described as "exceptional". It was a serious blow because the town had no other major industry to support trade and commerce. By the time the First World War ended, the number of animals appearing in St Ives in a year was less than the number that would have been shown on a single Monday in its heyday.

The gradual decline continued down the years, though for a short period there was a growth in the trade in pigs and poultry, and in the 1920s a substantial trade was established with London in these products. The market was once again hit badly during the Second World War, and was finally closed down in 1979.

Lincolnshire-born Joe Johnson, now 73, who came to St Ives in 1955 to become a partner in the auctioneering firm of Dilley, Theakston and Beardmore, presided over the last auction in March of that year. There were no cattle up for sale, the auction being confined to sheep and pigs.

Now living in Houghton, the retired auctioneer says: "I watched the cattle market dying. The final decline of the market came about because of the depreciation in profit from keeping livestock, and the trouble in finding labour to do weekend work. Eventually scientists discovered new fertilisers and sprays, and also discovered they could grow wheat in wheat or cereal upon cereal, and these products were much more profitable. They needed no manure, and so livestock in the area declined rapidly."

The firm Joe Johnson joined started out in 1830 as Fox. It was then taken over by James (Jas) Dilley, and later became Dilley and Son, and later Dilley Son and Read. Following an amalgamation it became Dilley, Theakston and Read, and when Read died, it became Dilley, Theakston and Beardmore. After a second amalgamation its name was changed to Ekins, Dilley and Handley. It was then sold to the Prudential Estate Agents.

At the height of its fame the market was a cosmopolitan place. While cattle were bought and sold in Broadway, sheep traded hands on Market Hill. The pig market was behind the White Hart and horses in Oliver Road and East Street. Poultry was sold in Crown Yard and the basket dealers were to be found at the top end of Bridge Street. Dairy products changed hands in Free Church Lane.

A newspaper account of the cattle market in the 1880s shows that it started at an early hour, and in the winter sales were completed by torchlight as the fatstock section would be nearly over by 6am. On Mondays droves of beasts could be seen being herded to Cambridge, St Neots and other towns an hour later. The English store cattle would be brought to market about 8am and the Irish animals by 9am. Some cattle salesmen would show more than 1,000 beasts, and droves of six, seven or even eight hundred were commonplace.

A number of family firms have been in business in the town for more than a century. Among them is the wine and spirit company now run by Rex Wadsworth and his son Steven. John Wadsworth combined with a man called Stocker in the 1830s to set up a mineral water and wine and spirit business. The partnership broke up after a few years and Wadsworth kept the aerated water part of the business. The factory was at the foot of the bridge leading into town.

John Wadsworth was Rex's great grandfather, and his son, Horatio took over the firm. Horatio used to go to Italy for voice training classes and was known as Horatio Summers when he appeared on concert platforms. The business then went to Rex's father, Guido, and his uncle Ernesto – their mother was French and had lived in Italy. Rex took it over in 1970.

In the 1960s the company added wines and spirits to their thriving mineral water trade and the firm claims to have one of the biggest selections of whisky in the country. They supply customers from as far away as Southampton and Scotland.

It was John Bryant who opened up a draper's shop in Bridge Street, a shop which is still in business in its original site. The brothers split up and Robert opened a men's wear shop on Market Hill. This too trades today. John Bryant's son, Douglas took over his father's shop, and it became a limited company in 1924. The present owner is David Bryant who joined the company in 1952.

Today the shop employs about 30 staff, but there was a time before ready made clothes became easily available when there would be 20 staff in the work room alone. Those were the days when any woman wanting a new outfit had to have it made, and the staff were kept busy running up dresses and coats for weddings, christenings and funerals.

Barton's chemist's shop in Bridge Street was established in 1820 by Thomas Prior. In 1869 he sold it to Henry Barton who managed it until his death in 1921. He was succeeded by his son, Frederick Cooke Barton and he in turn by his son Kenderick Michael Barton. When Michael Barton retired in 1987 the business was closed. The site was converted into flats, but the front of the shop was listed and survives. All the other nineteenth century shop fronts in Bridge Street have long since gone. On his retirement Michael Barton gave many of the shop items, including a large brass sign fitted under his shop's window, to the Norris Museum where they are on display.

He also gave the Museum his prescription books as well as old ledgers and notebooks. They give an insight into the workings of the business, and also furnish a glance at some of the medical histories of well known St Ivians. The names of some of the patent medicines which people swallowed in the last century are fascinating. A chemist's trade in the 1800s was far wider ranging than it is today, and Barton's sold wine and spirits to his customers as well as medicines. The Bartons in neat handwriting meticulously kept a record of all their transactions, and the ledgers disclose which of the wealthier residents of the town were considered credit-worthy to be able to run accounts both for their medications and their supplies of the hard stuff.

In 1877 we find a Mr Clemison of Cromwell Place, a regular customer for liquor. Every month he placed an order for cognac. In March that year when he ordered two bottles with the addition of a bottle each of sherry and port, he apparently also felt in need of a bottle of Barton's pills, a general tonic. Miss Cole of The Quay enjoyed a drop of wine or gin once in a while and each month would order either Marsala, Spanish Port or gin. She must have been very credit-worthy as she paid her bill once a year.

A William Viles was obviously a painter and decorator as he ordered large quantities of paint of all colours as well as turpentine. He also purchased boiled linseed oil in substantial quantities. A newspaper cutting attached to his last account shows that poor Mr Viles, who died in 1883, was declared a bankrupt the following year. He must have been one of Barton's debtors, as the notice in the paper calls on all those owed money by the dead man to file their claims before Cambridge's Official Receiver.

The borough council was a good customer. During 1877, a typical year, the local authority regularly bought MacDougall's powder, chloride of lime, disinfecting powder, Condy's Fluid, paints, oil, paint pots, paint brushes and putty.

Bartons appeared to supply the White Horse with all the soda water that public house required and they also kept Mr Macquire the boatwright going by selling him paint, oak stain, oak varnish and turpentine. Mr H. Golding the town crier in 1877 liked a drop of port or sherry, while when Mr Hopkins of the Bullock Market was not buying whisky, cognac, claret or gin, he would purchase paraffin and smelling salts.

Mr J. A. Hill, a modest drinker, enjoyed quinine wine and also worried about increasing baldness, for he is marked down for hair restorer and plenty of vaseline. On one occasion he bought a xylonite comb. Farmers provided Bartons with a steady income from the sale of sheep ointment and dog biscuits, while the family firm seems to have had a monopoly for supplying the British School with ink.

A Miss Egerton, whose address is not given because her account was in the name of Mrs Selwyn of Hemingford Abbots was apparently a semi-invalid. In March 1878 she ordered three lots of camphor, a box of salt lemon, iodine, hydrosulphic soda and mustard leaves. In April she required linament, Gray's powders, Holloway's ointment, lint, laudanum, Seidlitz powders and some unspecified pills.

Mr Holloway of Bridge Street regularly bought claret by the dozen, while animal lover

Mr Sheringham bought dog biscuits by the hundred weight. Mr Johnstone of the post office got through a bottle of claret practically every day. Every now and then Barton would write the word "bad" in large letters and underline it at the foot of an account, having presumably given up hope of being paid an amount that was not worth going to court for.

It is surprising to discover how much women, particularly lonely, unmarried ones, drank in the privacy of their homes. Poor Miss Clayton of East Street seemed to feel the need of a comforting glass daily. In the space of one month in 1886 she ordered seven bottles of brandy, and her other purchases that month included two lots of carbolic acid, Keatings insect powder, mustard, a bottle of castor oil and Higgins Enema. The ledger shows she continued to enjoy her brandy as the year wore on, but that the need for laxatives was over. Her purchases included tea and coffee, while she attended to her hygiene with the aid of Pears soap and a sponge. As the year drew to a close she began to supplement her brandy with the occasional bottle of sherry.

Local clergymen also enjoyed a relaxing drink. The Rev. J. R. Warburton's favourite tipples were port and cognac, though he once in a while would pour himself a whisky or a gin. The Rev J. Harrison from Wyton relied on Bartons for coconut oil, Condy's Fluid, hop bitters, cigarettes, matches and weed killer, and from time to time would ask for a bottle of whisky or invalid port. It seems the most favoured scotch in the town at the turn of the century was Glen Spey. Epsom salts and sulphur were much in demand as purgatives.

Mr Maskell of Hemingford Abbots must have been one of the outstanding hypocondriacs in the area, and he was a chemist's dream. His orders were packed with demands for Dill Water, Scotts pills, Steadman's powders, worm cakes, syrup of senna, syrup of rhubarb, Gosnells violet powders and camphor cakes, nearly all purgatives. He also trusted linseed oil and lavender water.

When Kiddle's shop was undertaking restoration work earlier this century, workmen made a curious find. Behind a wooden panel they came across a copy of a letter dated June 24, 1795 addressed to the Admiralty. It was unsigned and dealt with an engagement between British and French fleets off Minorca. It was after this skirmish that Admiral John Byng was shot for neglecting his duty. How the letter came to be on Kiddle's premises is not known, but the building was built for the Duke of Manchester who possibly entertained a naval officer at one time. The letter was sent on to the National Maritime Museum in London.

A business that used literally to contribute to the atmosphere of St Ives was the English Chicory Factory. Standing off Needingworth Road near the Manchester Arms, it only needed a north-east wind for the whole centre of St Ives to be filled with the smell of drying chicory. Chicory looks rather like a parsnip, and was used as an additive in some kinds of instant coffee. It is more bitter than real coffee, four times as strong and very much cheaper. It used to be grown in places all over the Fens and taken to the St Ives factory to be processed and dried.

Chapter 12
All Saints

The parish church of All Saints towers above the River Ouse and looks down upon the spot where the first Saxon pioneers pitched camp and established the tiny village of Slepe. It is mentioned in the Domesday Book, and was probably built on the site of an earlier chapel. The earliest existing portions date from the twelfth century, and the Early English window in the east end of the south aisle from the fourteenth.

Norris says the first authentic record about a parish church is contained in a document of 1251, which clearly states there were two churches in the settlement – a parish church and St Ivo's Priory. The entry reads: "By an inquisition taken in the 35th year of King Henry III, it was found that the parish church of St Ives, dedicated to the honour of All Saints, was a vicarage of the presentation of the abbot of Ramsey; that the prior of St Ives, as parson, received all the corn tithes, and the vicar, for his portion, £4.13s. 4d; that the vicar received all the small tithes, obventions, mortuaries, plough-alms, rates, and other customs too large here to be set down".

The church is a good specimen of the perpendicular style and with one exception all the windows are uniform. The building consists of a nave with clerestory, north and south aisles, chancel and porches. The nave is separated from the aisles by three pairs of clustered piers. The tower at the west end is supported by massive, well proportioned piers at its angles and is open to the aisles by pointed arches. It is topped by a spire which has been repeatedly rebuilt. The clock, with Handel's chimes, was manufactured by Gillett and Johnston of Croydon, and was installed in 1872.

Four times in its lifetime the spire has had to be restored. It was blown down in September 1741 and in 1822 had to be rebuilt for a second time. During alterations in the town centre in 1983, three broad, painted pieces of planking were discovered in the Merryland premises now occupied by the Premier Travel Group. Four bell ringers are depicted on the planks together with bell ropes and wheels. The ringers are wearing buckled shoes, knee breeches and shirts with cravats. Their hair falls below their ears. The costumes have been authentically dated to between 1740 and 1760. This clearly suggests that work was being carried out on the bell tower at about that time.

Pettis records how six bells were hung in the tower, and were taken down in 1723 to be recast, with added metal, as eight bells. The townspeople were dissatisfied with the result and took the bell founder, Henry Penn of Peterborough, to court. The case dragged on for four years, and was finally decided in Penn's favour. By now the bell founder was on his death bed but Pettis writes savagely that the luckless man's death was "no loss, he was a vile man and gave trouble wherever he was concarned".

Canon T. M. N. Owen, the author of a standard work on Huntingdonshire church bells, takes a more charitable view of Penn, and suggests that a dramatic legend concerning his death might be true. According to this legend, far from being on his death bed, Penn was in court when the verdict was announced. Elated by the result, he rushed from the courtroom, leapt on his horse and promptly collapsed and died. Canon Owen agrees that this spectacular exit may not be true, and that Pettis' more prosaic account is probably more accurate.

Regardless of the truth or otherwise of the legend, All Saints now had eight bells squeezed into a space originally built for six. Ringing them posed problems and the new bells were designed to chime to a new ringing technique requiring them to be swung through almost a full circle. Perhaps the extra vibrations and weight were too much for the spire, but the fact is that less than 20 years after the installation, the spire collapsed on September 8, 1741 during a gale.

It was replaced in 1748, but further rebuilding was necessary in 1822 and again in 1879. The bells were rehung in 1896, but the supporting structure was by then too weak to allow ringing, and the bells were silenced for some years. In 1930 they were recast yet again and rehung as the final stage of restoration after an aircraft crashed into the spire. The painted planks have the distinction of being the earliest representation existing of ordinary St Ivians.

The comparatively bare interior of the church was completely altered in the 1890s with the addition of a screen and an organ. Statues of saints were also placed on brackets on the nave piers. The brackets date from the fifteenth century and so the statues were probably replacements for earlier ones destroyed during the Reformation. This work was done by the noted church architect, Sir Ninian Comper.

The aircraft crash was the most spectacular incident to occur in St Ives during the First World War. On March 23rd, 1918, one week before the abolition of what was then called the Royal Flying Corps and less than eight months before the armistice, the spire of All Saints was demolished by an aircraft heading for nearby Wyton airfield.

One man who can vividly recall the crash is 87-year-old Freddy Favell, the long time assistant town clerk when St Ives had borough status. He was a 15-year-old boy scout at the time and was walking through the churchyard with other scouts when the plane crashed. He recalls: "It was 6.30pm and we were coming back through the churchyard. The father of one of the scouts was a verger and would have been ringing the bells for a service, but it was Lent so there was no service. We watched as the plane landed on the meadow opposite and a member of the RFC got out. He had come to St Ives for a Saturday night out. He was a sergeant. The pilot then turned the plane round, revved the engines and took off".

Freddy next remembers the following snatch of conversation between two of his colleagues: "He's going to hit the church". "Don't talk so bloody daft". "He bloody is". The scouts dived for cover as the plane sliced off about 30 feet of the spire. Masonry fell around them and though one large chunk fell near one of the boys, no one was hurt.

Freddy, a widower, who had to have a leg amputated while he was a young man and is now quite blind, continues: "It was very frightening. The plane did not seem to be in trouble, and it must have been a misjudgement. The plane went straight through the steeple and plunged vertically landing in the north aisle. The pilot was 19 years old and came from the Midlands. He died instantly but his watch was still working after the crash. Crowds soon gathered, but there was a danger of escaping gas following the impact and people living in the vicinity were warned not to light matches. Just before the crash we had sounded The Last Post at the end of one of our scout exercises".

A local newspaper described the scene at the time: "The pilot made a successful ascent and everything was apparently going well when, to the horror of many eyewitnesses, he dashed straight into the south side (of the church), cutting clean through the fabric some 30 feet from the top. The impact was terrible, the crash being heard for miles around, and the noise of the falling masonry instantly brought a large crowd on the scene.

"The pilot was killed instantly. On impact the steeple toppled over, the aircraft turned turtle and nose dived into the church which was fortunately empty at the time. A pack of boy scouts, passing through the churchyard, had to dive for cover. One of them was lying under a tree when a large coping stone landed inches away from him. The vicar, the Rev. Oscar Wilde, had left the church ten minutes before the crash occurred".

Many of the vestry books belonging to All Saints are now in the County Record Office at Huntingdon. They give an interesting, if fragmented account of the church's history. Included in the collection are some of the payment books of church officials in the early 1800s showing

Fig. 15. All Saints' church, photographed on 24th March 1918, the morning after the air crash; with Canon Ronald Jennings, vicar 1963–82, and Rev. David Moore, vicar since 1983.

the amounts paid out to the town's paupers during the second half of 1809. Every individual name is listed with the amounts paid weekly against each recipient's name. There are 115 names. The majority of the allowances range from one shilling to five shillings a week, though widow Legett was receiving six shillings, and during the last four months of the year widow Newman, who had been receiving six shillings, had an increase to seven.

The books also refer to the plane crash. They state: "The nave roof had several holes made in it. The bells were hurled to the belfry floor, and much of the carved oak used for seats was smashed as were many of the marble monuments. Memorial tablets were also damaged, and the figure of Mary Magdalene on one of the nave pillars was thrown to the floor. The organ was choked with dust and debris. With the church out of action, the Bishop of Ely licensed the Ramsey Road school for religious services".

The church was insured by the Ecclesiastical Insurance Office against damage by "aerial aircraft, hostile or otherwise", for £14,000. After a government inspector had surveyed the damage, a London architect and the Cambridge building firm of W. Saint Ltd were asked to undertake a survey and submit estimates for the repair work. Architect J. N. Coupe reported that the roof over the nave and also above the north and south aisles had been so severely damaged and had, in any case, before the crash been in such poor condition, that simply to reconstruct them and to patch them up would be unsatisfactory. He strongly urged new roofs.

The cost of rebuilding the spire with repairs to the tower and all the work involved in re-roofing together with work inside the church would be about £7,090. Inspector Burnet Brown agreed with Coupe, but said the government would pay only half the total cost of restoration. After talks which lasted more than six months, the government agreed to pay £3,783.15s. A meeting on October 16th 1918 approved all the plans and in November an appeal for funds was launched.

A Thanksgiving service was held on March 24th, 1928 to mark the completion of the work. It was two and a half years later before the eight bells were finally recast and rehung and the newly repaired clock installed. The church was back to normal more than a dozen years after an inexperienced fighter pilot made his fatal error of judgement. The total cost had been £12,757.2s.10d. The vicar at the reopening in 1928 was the Rev. Oscar Wilde.

In a very early minute book dated 1634, Oliver Cromwell's signature appears alongside a vestry minute. At that time his signature was written in a small, almost timid looking hand, quite unlike the florid signature that rounded off subsequent decrees issued when he was Lord Protector. In 1635 the St Ives farmer once more had occasion to sign his name in the minute book. This time the blameless signature was not to be left to the gaze of future historians. There is a tear in the page, and some later vicar has written by the damaged spot: "OC writes name here but cut out supposed by John Bently in 1732, he then churchwarden. No thanks for it".

All Saints has known some colourful characters. One of these was Dr John Hunt, who was appointed curate of All Saints in 1865, served under vicar Yate Fosbrooke, and was dismissed by the latter's successor, the Rev. Charles Goldie. After his dismissal, the sacked curate, a man of pronounced religious views and also a wry sense of humour, published an account of his stay at St Ives.

It was published as a pamphlet in 1867, and Hunt went to extreme lengths to provide anonymity. He referred to the town as Ousebank, and altered the names of all those people he mentioned. He signed his pamphlet "A Presbyter". This laudable attempt to mislead his readers was thwarted by his wife, who scribbled the real names in the margins of one copy of the pamphlet. This is now in the library of the Norris Museum.

Dr Hunt was obviously not an easy man with whom to work. His relations with the vicar began on an excellent footing, but Fosbrooke, who gloried in being "a gentleman" and had a somewhat simplistic approach to the bible, began to suspect his curate of harbouring unorthodox views. At times the two men came near to falling out, which was socially awkward as Hunt lived with the Rev. Fosbrooke and his wife in the vicarage.

The pamphlet is entertaining reading. Some may feel that in parts it is bitter to the point of being spiteful. But in general Hunt comes across as a courteous man who never actually bore malice towards his vicar.

Hunt arrived to discover that his superior was a high minded man, and it was not long before he heard his vicar describe himself, as he frequently did, as "a gentleman, born a gentleman who has always associated with gentlemen". He was a somewhat unfortunate choice for vicar in a town which contained a strong and active body of dissenters.

Hunt paints a vivid picture of the Rev. Fosbrooke, using the pseudonym "Mr. Coldstream". He writes: "Mr. Coldstream had been vicar of Ousebank nearly 30 years. He was an old fashioned clergyman, and was proud of his office not so much for the office itself, but because an English clergyman was equivalent to an English gentleman. A clergyman of the church of England and an old English gentleman were to him nearly the same, and each was the ideal pre-eminently of all that was great, good and desirable in this mortal life.

"His ancestors had been clergymen since the days of Charles I. They had stood by the Stuarts in adversity as well as in prosperity. His father was an eminent scholar, but Mr. Coldstream himself had no pretensions to learning. It was enough for him to be a gentleman".

The vicar used to boast of the numerous invitations he received "to brilliant dinners out while but a curate", and while at Cheltenham in that humble capacity, he evidently was the darling of social hostesses, never slow to be the first on the ballroom floor. In his old age he was apt to recall with some bitterness that frequent promises of preferment extended by dukes, lords and bishops in the gilded atmosphere of his youth had come to nothing, and that he was ending his days as a vicar in a rural town.

Hunt found his new church an impressive building, and its spire he described as "the very perfection of symmetry". At first the two men got on well. The vicar was impressed by his new curate's sermons. Soon after Hunt's arrival he told him: "There is a great opinion of your talents abroad in the town. Your sermons are the subject of conversation everywhere". By this time the curate had realised there was a large religious divide in St Ives. Apart from the parish church there were half a dozen meeting houses as well as the imposing Free Church on Market Hill.

The vicar had literally bought his living. This was an accepted practice in the nineteenth century, and he felt he could exercise *droit de seigneur* over the parish. As Hunt writes: "He had bought the temporalities and the spiritualities of Ousebank. Dissenters were interfering with HIS rights. They were HIS parishioners, and it was THEIR duty to submit to him in all things". This patrician attitude did not endear Fosbrooke to those St Ivians who worshipped elsewhere than in All Saints. When he attempted to impose a church rate to be paid by all residents of the town, he faced fierce opposition and was eventually defeated. Angry meetings were held by non-anglicans. There were stormy exchanges of correspondence in local newspapers. The town was a hubbub of controversy and in the end the proposed rate was never levied.

The honeymoon between Fosbrooke and Hunt lasted barely a year. By 1866 the vicar began to question the orthodoxy of the man whose early sermons he had extravagantly praised. Hunt preached what he termed "practical religion". His vicar suggested he should start preaching "church doctrine". Fosbrooke was also suspicious of some of the books Hunt read, and described the author of a book on Judaism as "that infidel." Hunt had his own subtle way of getting his own back. After listening to a tirade about sermons being preached in Brighton by the Rev. Frederick Robertson, he asked Fosbrooke what he had thought of a sermon his curate had recently preached in All Saints.

"It was one of the best sermons you have preached in Ousebank", the vicar replied.

"Between you and I", Hunt remarked, "that sermon was Frederick Robertson's. I sometimes preach other people's sermons just to see how my own stand beside them".

There came a point at which Fosbrooke became convinced his curate was not a "sound churchman". A strange relationship then grew between the two men. They frequently discussed dogma, and however excited or sarcastic the vicar became, Hunt claims he himself always spoke civilly and did not allow his temper to get the better of his tongue. Hunt began to believe the vicar would like him to leave the parish, but when it became clear he intended to remain, Fosbrooke appeared to accept his continuing presence without rancour.

Fosbrooke had for some time suffered from a cardiac disorder, but in the spring of 1866 his health appeared to be improving. He had been told by his doctors to give up, or at least to cut down on his preaching because the pressure involved was dangerous. At just about the same time he had become extremely irritable when he discovered that the patrons of the parish, who were obviously lacking in sensitivity, were advertising the living for sale.

Enquiries about the living kept being made at the vicarage where they were testily brushed aside. Fosbrooke told enquirers he had taken on a new lease of life, that he had no intention of dying, and that the parish would not be requiring a new incumbent for some years. This assertion proved to be inaccurate.

Soon afterwards the diocesan bishop gave notice he would be arriving in St Ives to conduct a confirmation service. The vicar energetically threw himself into the preparations for the visit, inviting everyone wanting to be confirmed to come to his vicarage where he personally would instruct them. Between 40 and 50 young parishioners responded, were formed into classes, and taught by Fosbrooke two to three nights a week.

The confirmation service sparked the last disagreement between vicar and curate. Fosbrooke reproached Hunt for not being active enough in the preparations and said he should be going around the town to "beat up candidates for the confirmation". Hunt was appalled. "Beat up candidates for confirmation", he exclaimed. "I do not know what that means. I never did such a thing, and I never will. We should present to the bishop such persons as we know are prepared to receive confirmation and not go through the parish to beat them up for a few weeks before the bishop comes".

Whether the enthusiasm with which Fosbrooke had thrown himself into the preparations for the bishop's visit had been ill advised, or whether there was some other cause, the vicar was taken ill within a fortnight of the service. The doctors forbade him to preach at all and, as their patient's condition deteriorated, told him to prepare for the end. "He might linger for a while, but there would be no recovery".

After this sentence of death Fosbrooke confined himself to his vicarage where he slowly grew weaker. The living was now clearly up for sale, and Hunt, who had no private means, could have acquired it when a friend of his in London offered to buy it and install him as the new vicar. Hunt showed his sensitivity when he refused the offer. In his pamphlet he wrote: "My whole being recoiled at the thought of buying the presentation while Mr. Coldstream lay on his death bed. The charge of the souls of a parish is responsibility enough in itself, without adopting underhand ways of procuring it". He knew that when the living came to be publicly advertised, it would go to the highest bidder, and for far more than his friend could afford.

It was July 1866, the vicarage garden was in full bloom and Fosbrooke who had always taken a keen interest in gardening, would sit for hours at a window looking at the flowers, shrubs and trees. He would also watch the birds and took a particular interest in a pair of longbills who, for several summers had nested and raised their young in his garden.

He met his death with dignity. One morning he said farewell to his closest friends. That afternoon he died. A sobbing housemaid ran into Hunt's study with the news. About an hour later the curate claims, he went for a walk in the garden and looked for the longbills. He says he found them all dead in their nest.

Hunt went on to run the parish temporarily, and a churchwarden was appointed

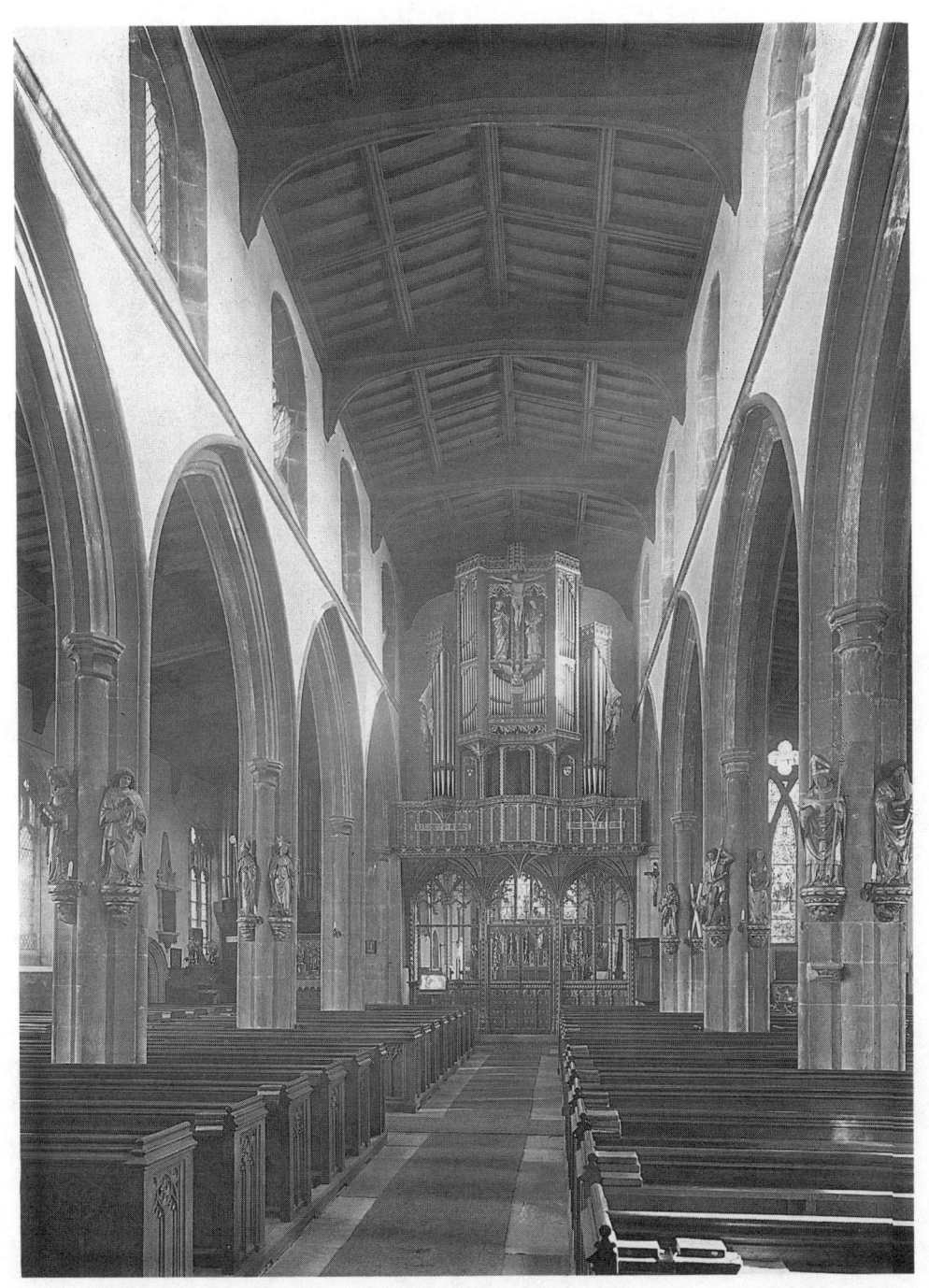

Fig. 16. The interior of All Saints, showing the statues and organ screen designed by Sir Ninian Comper.

sequestrator to administer church finances until a new vicar was appointed. There was much speculation as to who this man would be and several names were bandied about. Hunt's name was not among them. Though he was very popular, the parishioners knew the patrons would pick someone with private means, a man who would pay towards church maintenance and restoration jobs.

The curate noted sadly: "By every law of equity and propriety the living of Ousebank should have been given to me. This was the all but universal wish of the people . . . but the patrons wished it to be sold to someone who could spend something upon it".

After several weeks the living was offered to the Rev. Charles Goldie who was said to have a private income of £2,000 a year, as well as 22 children. The Primitive Methodist butcher and the Particular Baptist grocer could not conceal their delight upon hearing the news. In fact the size of Goldie's income as well as that of his family had been exaggerated, in the case of his family, grossly so. Goldie at first turned down the invitation but subsequently accepted it. There had been rumours that he was a high churchman. Quite how high was soon to become apparent.

Hunt writes: "We had always passed in Ousebank for being a little high church. But Mr. Goldwing (Goldie) surprised us all. He was no Jesuit introducing things by stealth. He was no man of half measures". The new vicar quickly introduced extreme high church forms of service. Some of these offended members of his congregation, but it was generally agreed he was a man who would devote himself to the good of his parish. Still, the choir boys and some members of his congregation had difficulty in concealing their amusement when Goldie first began bobbing about the altar and genuflecting.

During his first week Goldie wrote to the curate enclosing a form. This would normally have set out the new arrangements between a new vicar and an established curate. In this case it was a note of dismissal. Goldie explained this summary sacking by saying he had received copies of two sermons preached by the doctor since Fosbrooke's death.

His letter continued: "According to my view they are in parts so lamentably deficient in the full statement of truth, and in some parts so erroneous, that I feel it my duty either personally or by deputy to supply your place in the pulpit during the next six weeks. I shall be glad to have your assistance in the reading desk and otherwise".

After offering to discuss points of dogma with Hunt to see whether he could iron out his religious views, the vicar concluded somewhat piously: "I hope that the fact of my acting thus will not in any way destroy our friendly converse during the short remainder of our connection". Goldie later said Hunt was guilty of diverging from "catholic truth".

To this attack Hunt made a dignified reply. He said he had no wish to remain in the parish as his vicar had identified himself "with a party in the church with whose peculiar views I have no sympathy in the world". After this swipe at Goldie's high church leanings, the curate said he appreciated that the vicar would prefer a curate who shared his views.

He continued: "But to inhibit me from the pulpit is an arbitary and uncalled for exercise of power, likely, I fear, to recoil upon yourself. . . . not to allow me to preach a final sermon is to make me a martyr when I do not wish to be one".

After defending his sermons and musing on the meaning of Catholic truth, Hunt allowed himself two sentences of anger. "There is no such thing (as Catholic truth) in the sense in which you seem to use the words", he said. "There are Catholic lies in abundance, Catholic errors and Catholic superstitions which must be swept away with the besom of destruction".

Having vented his frustration he ended on a conciliatory note, saying he would do nothing during the rest of his stay which might endanger "a friendly understanding between us".

The matter did not end there. Goldie had started a hare which intended to run. The bishop of Ely was not too pleased about the pulpit ban, local newspapers reported it prominently with the result that Hunt's two sermons which had so offended Goldie were printed and sold several hundred copies.

Goldie meanwhile was busy writing explanatory letters to outraged parishioners and for some reason ignored his churchwardens. The unfortunate sequestrator who some years earlier had unwisely married his dead wife's sister under a more benign regime, felt the lash of the new one. Goldie denied him the sacraments. The parish was troubled and walls in the town were plastered with posters demanding "No Popery". Letters from anglicans filled columns in the newspapers.

One morning Hunt, sitting in his study, heard the town crier declaiming: "This is to give notice that whosoever enters a dissenting place of worship commits an offence against God. These are the words spoken in the parish church of Ousebank on Sunday morning last, and he who said them is a liar and a fool".

One suspects that Hunt, despite his courteous protestations, derived quiet pleasure from the uproar his sacking had set in motion. Could he even have played a subtle hand in starting it? Anyone reading the full text of his pamphlet can scarcely come away without suspecting a sardonic, even wicked sense of humour.

The curate left while the argument was raging. Goldie wisely lifted his ban at the last moment and Hunt preached one final sermon. "There was not much wrong with Mr. Goldwing", he later confided to his diary, "except the poison of the pernicious nonsense. Sacerdotal blood flowed in his arteries, and filled his veins to repletion".

On the Friday before his departure a crowd packed the Corn Exchange. Hunt was presented with 30 guineas in a long purse with dazzling tassels. The chairman made a speech in which he referred to the curate as "a talented preacher and a great scholar". Hunt replied with a speech in which he ranged over his experiences in St Ives and in which he expounded his religious beliefs at some length.

It is interesting to speculate on the reason behind Goldie's lightning dismissal of Hunt. Had he been warned before his arrival that his curate was a singularly independent man, and so had resolved to get rid of him without delay? Two sermons from a preacher widely respected locally, no matter how offensive to Goldie, seemed hardly a valid reason for so swift a *coup de grace*.

On the other hand Hunt emerges from the pages of his pamphlet as a polite but prickly man, an evasive man, clever enough to cloak his deeds with diplomatic words. In Goldie he came up against a vicar strongly drawn towards Rome, to whom Hunt's practical approach to religion would have been distasteful. The patrician but tolerant Fosbrooke had had his ups and downs with Hunt but basically had been able to get along with him. Goldie was a different matter. Inevitably, Goldie's time as vicar of All Saints was marked by periodic clashes with the nonconformists. If Fosbrooke could be considered a perilous choice to represent anglicanism in a strongly nonconformist town, the selection of Goldie could be viewed as even more dangerous. Goldie's son John became a local hero when he stroked Cambridge to three victories in the University boat race, breaking a string of Oxford successes. Cambridge University's second boat is named Goldie in his honour.

In the mid 1870s the vicar came into open confrontation with the Rev. Thomas Lloyd, the minister of the Free Church, over the respective running of British schools controlled by nonconformists, and of National schools, run by the Anglican church.

The vicar campaigned for all schools to be run by the newly established School Board. The legislation setting up this body did not compel schools to invite the board to take over. Goldie, however, no doubt with an eye to an influential role on the local Board, agitated for the taking over by the Board of the British school in St Ives.

He accused its administrators of overspending and slack management. This drew an immediate response in the form of a pamphlet written by Lloyd, the man who had been largely responsible for building the present Free Church. He rebutted Goldie's accusations and derided Goldie's neo-Catholic beliefs. He alleged that all Goldie was after was control of the School Board, and that if he achieved this aim, he would ensure that children of nonconformist parents would be taught high church doctrines. In the end the School Board took over the running of both schools.

In 1931 another powerful, charismatic figure swept into the enormous, rambling vicarage. William Strowon Amherst Robertson, universally known with affection as Father Algy, had been born into a wealthy family at Ealing in 1894. Archbishop William Temple once remarked of him: "No, I don't know Father Robertson, but I do, of course, know Algy". Robertson was a boy at Westminster when he acquired the nickname which stuck to him for the rest of his life.

He replaced as vicar of All Saints the Rev. Oscar Wilde, a somewhat aloof character who was intensely proud of being related to his notorious namesake. A pale, bespectacled man, Father Algy was a delicate child. In 1917, after graduating from Cambridge, he was appointed professor of English literature at St Paul's College, Calcutta. A strong anglo-catholic, he returned to this country in 1920, but was determined to return to India, a country with which he had fallen in love.

His stomach had always been suspect, and being made a Travelling Secretary for the Student Christian Movement, did not aid his digestion, as it was an exacting job. In 1922 there had been inaugurated in the central Indian town, a movement named Christa Sera Sangha, the Society of Servants belonging to Christ. Its adherents took vows of poverty, celibacy and obedience. There were initially six brethren, five Indian and their Superior or Acharya, Father Jack Winslow, who had gone to India before the outbreak of the 1914 war. The brethren wore cassocks of white homespun cloth with a saffron girdle. Saffron was the traditional colour of renunciation in India. Members of the society were vegetarians and their mission was to minister to the poor.

Winslow met Father Algy on a visit to England, and the latter agreed to join the Sangha with a group of friends. Even at this early stage Father Algy apparently foresaw that the Sangha would be the basis for a group of Franciscan Friars. In 1927 he joined the Sangha in Poona. For a brief period he was blissfully happy, but the climate and the food proved too much for his ravaged stomach and he was constantly ill. In 1930 doctors told him he must leave India and never return.

This news came as a dreadful blow to the earnest missionary. On his return to England he was treated at the London School for Tropical Diseases and then needed a long convalescence. It was at this point that the Rev. Oscar Wilde retired from All Saints. Father Algy was offered the living, declined it, but accepted when the offer was repeated.

He came into the vicarage armed with a new broom, and the broom swept clean. Wilde had been a remote, patrician figure, in some ways a replica of Fosbrooke. He regarded himself as a gentleman, and he and his wife lived in style at the vicarage. The gates were only opened when one of them drove out or returned home. They maintained a staff of servants.

This lifestyle did not suit Father Algy. Most of the servants went, the vicarage gates were thrown open. The new incumbent hoped to establish an organisation called the Brotherhood of Love of Christ with Christa Sera Sangha as its inspiration. Parishioners gaped as the new vicar threw himself with boundless energy into his new plans. He filled the grounds of the vicarage with young men, many of them coloured, who had been drawn by the sheer force of his personality to help him.

In church Father Algy maintained the splendour of the services for which Wilde had been renowned, but he encouraged his young parishioners to come to the vicarage where the doors of all the rooms, except those of his study, were always open. He turned lawns into tennis courts and ordered life within the vicarage on lines adapted from the Sangha. Novices wore the saffron girdle of renunciation. Amidst what appeared to be chaos he established the third

Franciscan Brotherhood in the country, the other two being at Cerne Abbas in Dorset and Peckham in London.

All the while his tortured stomach played him up. Today he would have been prescribed drugs to ease the pain, but half a century ago he was on his own. He took to strapping a hot water bottle beneath his cassock which made him a figure of fun for some people. As he dashed from appointment to appointment or charged around the vicarage organising this that and the other, the water confined to the bottle strapped round his waist would go glug, glug, glug. Mary Grove and Ethel Cuttill are among those still living in St Ives who can remember this bustling figure with the hypnotic light blue eyes and the ability to inspire great loyalty and affection. Some of his mean minded colleagues sneered behind his back at his family's wealth. They whispered that it was easy enough for him to take luxurious short breaks. Whenever his pains became unbearable, Father Algy would take the train to London where his mother would make sure there was a car at Kings Cross to take him to her home. Father Algy would emerge from these breaks refreshed and would throw himself with ever greater energy into his goal of promoting his fellowship.

In 1936 he was transferred to Cerne Abbas as Novice Master, though he officially remained vicar of All Saints for another year. In the end his stomach could take no more. By 1955 he was in such poor health he had at times to be supported up and down stairs. He died that year in a London hospital.

In 1963 an urbane cleric with an unusual background was appointed to All Saints. Canon Ronald Jennings had been archdeacon of The Gambia before coming to St Ives. He retired in December 1982. Born and bred in Worcestershire, he now lives in retirement at Pinchbeck in Lincolnshire. He is still active in the church, doing a week's duty at a time in Westminster Abbey, and day duties at St Pauls and at Peterborough cathedrals. He is also an enthusiastic worker for funds for The Gambia. A bachelor, he recalls his days at St Ives with great affection and describes it as "the happiest period of my life".

His successor is the Rev. David Moore who arrived from Nuneaton in April 1983. Yorkshire born, he was ordained in 1956. He is married and has five grown-up children. A man with a laid-back manner, when he first arrived he was struck with a difference he noted between St Ives and Nuneaton. In his Warwickshire parish, nearly all his parishioners were involved in either the hosiery or motor trades. This common denominator made for a closely knit community. In St Ives he found a parish embracing a congregation drawn from all walks of life.

"It is a transient parish," he observes. "St Ives has become to some degree a commuter's dormitory. People live here and work in London, Cambridge or Peterborough. I also get service families coming to the church for the first time. You get to know them and then they move away. But I find it an interesting place in which to work".

Chapter 13
Nonconformity in St Ives

St Ives has a long tradition of nonconformity. During the Civil War the town was in Roundhead hands and it escaped the fate of Huntingdon which, for a short spell, was the scene of bloody fighting between the royalists and the parliamentary forces. In the case of religion this independent trait is also evident. St Ives was a breeding ground for Dissenters in the seventeenth century, and at one time, in addition to the Free Church, Methodist and Baptist congregations that worshipped here, there were several other meeting houses.

Mary Carter, a teacher at St Peter's School, Huntingdon, has traced the formation and development of the Free Church in the town in her book, *Not an Easy Church*, published in 1982. Her researches show that the first major step towards establishing a nonconformist congregation took place 19 years before Oliver Cromwell arrived to farm in St Ives. In 1612 a puritan, the Rev. Job Tookey, was appointed vicar of All Saints.

Two differing portraits of Tookey have been painted. In one set of letters he is depicted as a humble, holy man, who took the communion bread to members of his congregation as they sat in their pews. Some reports say he was thrown out of St Ives in 1630 for refusing to read the Book of Sports, which listed those leisure activities which were permitted on Sundays, as he was against all forms of recreation on the sabbath.

Another set of letters describes him as little more than a gullible old fool, who was rebuked by the Bishop of Lincoln after he had taken seriously the so called "revelations" of a girl pedlar named Jane Hawkins. This young woman, who was later unmasked as a trickster, kept going into a trance and mumbling her "revelations" in doggerel verse. Tookey took down all she said and appeared to believe what the woman was saying. The bishop declared that the whole affair was a hoax, and had some tart things to say to Tookey, who left the parish abruptly in 1630.

The new vicar was Henry Downhale who struck up a friendship with Cromwell. This was surprising, as the new incumbent was a fervent royalist who was to pay for his loyalty to the Stuarts during the Civil War. By this time Cromwell was well on the way not only to becoming a puritan, but was also questioning the position of the monarchy. The farmer began preaching his own brand of Christianity not only in his farmhouse, but also in the homes of his friends, one of whom was probably Dr Robert Wilde. He also invited outside preachers to the town. Soon after Cromwell left for Ely, the parishioners of All Saints complained to the Archbishop of Canterbury about the type of service being held in All Saints. They said they would not go to the altar to receive communion. The archdeacon of Huntingdon investigated this complaint and said they must go up to the altar.

After much argument a puritan lecturer was appointed to All Saints. He was John Tookey, the son of Job Tookey. Downhale was arrested and stripped of his living when the civil war broke out, and spent the next few years preaching to royalist forces. The Restoration brought the persecution of the puritans, and nonconformists risked fines and imprisonment. There are no actual records of these in St Ives, but we know that some Quakers were fined for refusing to attend church.

Tobias Hardmeat of Fenstanton, was not only fined, but also imprisoned more than once for this offence and also for not paying church tithes. This persecution stopped briefly when Charles II gave licences to Dissenters to preach and to hold meetings, but this proved to be a brief period of tolerance. In the following year he had to revoke the licences as they had not received parliamentary approval. In the meantime Obadiah Gee had been permitted to hold Presbyterian meetings in St Ives, and the first meeting house was founded in 1672. By 1672 the nonconformists in the town included the Presbyterians, the Baptists and the Quakers.

A survey in 1676 showed that 800 people attended the parish church while there were nearly 50 nonconformists. There were no Roman Catholics. By 1687 the nonconformists were well established and the Presbyterians had their own minister, the Rev. Robert Billio. The reign of William and Mary witnessed the passing of the Toleration Act. Under this nonconformists could hold meetings anywhere, providing the doors were open so that the police or government spies could get in. Tradition has it that the great fire of 1689 destroyed the Presbyterian meeting house on the Quay. This could have been Gee's house. There is a record that a new meeting place was built by 1691, by which time there were two nonconformist ministers in St Ives. The congregation had grown considerably, but both men had to preach elsewhere to supplement their incomes.

In 1709 we know that the Presbyterian church stood on the west side of what is now Free Church Passage on the site of the present premises of Fishes Galore and not far from the butchers' shops which were located on the edge of Market Hill. During subsequent reconstruction work the bones of many animals were unearthed. Records show that two children, one of them named Ephraim White, were buried in the meeting house. Their graves have never been discovered.

Presbyterians observed a very strict sabbath. The morning service would last for at least two hours, and many in the congregation took notes of the sermon. In the evening, relatives and friends would be invited over and the sermon would be discussed at length. Children were questioned on it. The entire day was devoted to prayers and devout conversation.

By 1715 the Presbyterian congregation numbered 500, but the parish church conducted three times as many baptisms. The reason for this was that a baptism certificate signed by the parish priest was necessary for any government post or for entry into the army or navy. This rule was strictly enforced, so that many nonconformists had their children baptised in a church at which they themselves did not worship. In 1811 it was decided to build a new brick chapel on the same site. When the building was completed it was named the Independent Chapel, marking its complete break with the anglican church and its financial independence. The building cost £1,155 which was borrowed and paid off in five years.

In the early part of the nineteenth century one of the most active lay preachers in the area was Potto Brown, a wealthy miller who rented a mill and farm at Houghton from Lady Olivia Sparrow. Brown had great influence in St Ives and attended the Presbyterian services there. A formidable man with great strength of character, Brown is something of an enigma. He gave freely to charity and was a good employer, but he was also a stern man with rigid rules of personal conduct which he tended to apply to the behaviour of others.

A dominant personality, he was generally the leader in anything he undertook, and must have been a difficult man to live with. His punctuality was legendary. Both his sons wrote about him after his death, and both C. P. Tebbutt, a prominent local nonconformist, and Robert Walker Dixon, a close personal friend, have left behind their recollections of Potto Brown.

This stern disciplinarian was well into middle age before he finally became a member of the Free Church. His uncharacteristic indecisiveness in this matter may have been due to his upbringing. He was brought up a Quaker, a movement which gave great religious freedom to its adherents. Each Quaker spoke to God in his own way. Quakers would gather in silence and they avowed a fundamental doctrine – each member was to be prompted and guided by the leading of the Holy Spirit. They called themselves the Society of Friends, and they could be intensely individualistic. Brown's family had been Quakers for generations and they believed that whatever else might have to be sacrificed, it must never be principle.

Quakers dressed simply and used the "thee" and "thou" in everyday conversation. Brown had the injunction "do right" drilled into him as a child, and he abided by it. He was born on July 16th, 1797 in Houghton.

As a child he attended the Friends' meeting house in St Ives. After school he assisted his father in the family mill until 1822 when his father retired. He continued with the mill and took as his partner Joseph Goodman. In 1822 he married Mary Bateman, a Quakeress from Chatteris. A man of enquiring mind, Brown began to have doubts about Quakerism and sought advice from a Quaker he held in high esteem. Instead of counselling the young man sympathetically, this patriarch administered a sharp rebuke. During the next few years Brown was from time to time censured by the local Friends for what his colleagues regarded as indiscipline, and in June 1837 he was formally disowned.

He then began worshipping at the Independent Chapel in St Ives, but did not greatly warm to the sermons of the minister, the Rev. Isaiah Knowles Holland, an erect, soldierly figure who had served in the army and was reported to have fought at Waterloo. A clever man, he preached intellectual, philosophical sermons, but lacked warmth, a quality Brown admired.

He started going in the afternoons to the anglican service in Hemingford Abbots where the clergyman was an evangelical and a friend of his. He took with him on his visits all his workers from the mill, much to the annoyance of Edward Martin Peck, the rector of Houghton, who stood fuming at a window of his rectory with his eye pressed against a telescope counting the number of his parishioners who were defecting.

At one point Brown decided to join the Church of England, but his efforts to work with the local clergy if not exactly rebuffed, were not too warmly welcomed. He built a chapel at Houghton and from then on attended three services every Sunday. At St Ives in the morning, at Hemingford Abbots in the afternoon and in his own village in the evening. His stern views on religion are illustrated by his attitude to the annual Houghton Fair. This was probably a perfectly innocent affair, but Brown disliked some of its features such as the dancing booths and the amount of alcohol consumed. He countered by setting up a large tent holding 300 and inviting well known temperance preachers to the village. There would be cricket, football and other games, but Kiss in the Ring was banned. Brown was a strict teetotaller. At home he had the quaint custom of only offering alcohol to anyone over the age of 60.

There had long been a Baptist congregation in the town whose roots were in Fenstanton. The Baptists built a chapel in St Ives in 1805 behind the Golden Lion. By 1860 they were in financial difficulties and unable to maintain a minister. After discussions lasting many months, they merged with the Independent Chapel and, despite initial frictions, the union was successful.

It was now decided to build a more impressive church and a building committee was set up which included the ubiquitous but religiously indecisive Brown. Land facing on to Market Hill where the shops of a baker, brewer and a cooper stood was bought for £1,500 including £100 to the Duke of Manchester which gave the new owners the freehold. The entire cost of the project was £5,150 which did not include furniture and fittings. Brown contributed £3,000 towards the cost and other worshippers chipped in. The church was left to raise £1,000. It was decided that the new name would be the Free Church. The foundation stone was laid in October 1863, and the work was completed in less than a year. The new building was dedicated on September 17th, 1864. It held 750 people.

It has been alleged that Brown laid down one condition before contributing his £3,000, that the spire of the new church must be two feet higher than that of All Saints. This seems highly unlikely in view of the former Quaker's attitude towards religious worship. Brown disliked stained glass windows, and the thought of the Free Church spire dominating the landscape for miles around would not have appealed to him.

When the chapel was dedicated, he boycotted the ceremony. His biographers have skirted over this, not dwelling upon it at all. But there can be no other reason for his absence on the great day other than a wish to express his displeasure. Had he been away on business, it would be inconceivable that he would not have arranged to be back in time for the ceremony.

Brown did not voice his reservations publicly for fear of putting off young people from going to worship, but privately he admitted to being troubled. Although he also had reservations about organ music, he did not oppose its introduction. Privately he would joke with the leader of the choir: "I can't think why you make so much of music, it's such a sensual thing. It's like having your ears tickled". Brown was unmusical, and what a psychiatrist would make of that remark, does not bear thinking about.

Brown ran his household on strict lines. Unpunctual visitors and guests received a frosty reception. He had some curious habits. Every Sunday morning he breakfasted off two eggs in the firm belief that they contained phosphorus which, he maintained, nourished the brain. He finally joined the Free Church soon after the opening of the new building. In 1859, now a widower, he remarried. His bride was the widow of a Chelmsford man, and the marriage was happy. His son, Bateman, became a justice of the peace and wrote several lengthy articles for the Peterborough Advertiser in 1905, and in the same year published his reminiscences. The early part of his book is mainly devoted to an account of his father's life.

When he donated £3,000 to the St Ives church, Potto Brown gave an identical amount for a church in Huntingdon. Trinity Church was even more ornate than the one in St Ives. Dixon records the doubts these two buildings planted in the benefactor's mind. He writes: "In providing this money, it was not part of his plan to develop the spires and ornaments but, having provided all the money necessary for simple, commodious chapels, he left others to carry out the manner of the expenditure". Others held different views. They felt the new churches must be grand, to signify the importance of the Dissenters. But the old man whose generosity largely made possible the building of the churches, never altogether jettisoned his old Quaker beliefs in the simplicity and austerity of religion.

New members began flocking in after the church was dedicated but the elders were alarmed when a Mr and Mrs Wilson chose to opt out. Their alarm chiefly concerned the unusual reason for the request for cancellation of membership. Mr Wilson wrote: "I now believe that God has created and has foredoomed by far the largest part of the human race to destruction and that none will be saved but the elect who are few in number". He went on to say he had reached the comforting conclusion that he and his wife were among the elect, and that as the rest of the congregation were doomed, he wanted nothing to do with them.

This high minded certainty of salvation, together with the clearly expressed belief that his fellow worshippers were sinners beyond redemption was hard to swallow. At any rate the deacons arranged that three "visitors" should meet the Wilsons to try to persuade them to remain. They doubtless hoped that Wilson would retract his letter, or at any rate that part of it which consigned the rest of the congregation, the deacons included, to damnation. But the Wilsons were obdurate and withdrew from membership.

Nonconformists felt deeply about the "correctness" of certain things. When the Rev. J. Hutchison married a woman many years younger than himself, eyebrows were raised. He might have survived, but when in 1903, he compounded his "offence" by announcing that he had resigned to join the Church of England, his departure from St Ives was swift. After he left his photograph was not placed alongside that of his predecessors.

The next year the church embarked upon an unsettling period. In 1904 the Rev. Albert Hooper was appointed minister. A man of fragile health, he lived a quiet life. A local writer says of him: "he was, from his earliest years, precluded by intense neuralgia, from all outdoor exercise or amusement, and he cultivated the literary side of his nature".

Several ministers attended his induction, including the Rev. R. J. Campbell from the City Temple, London. This minister was a leading exponent of the New Theology which was gaining adherents throughout the country. It exerted a large influence on the new minister.

Fig. 17. The architect's design for the Free Church, built 1863–64; with Rev. John Ballard, minister 1949–74, and Rev. Donald McIlhagga, minister since 1975, with Rev. Kate McIlhagga, community minister.

New Theology has been described as "the name given to a movement at the end of the nineteenth century which flourished until about the beginning of the Second World War. There already had been many changes in the climate of thought in the nineteenth century, but two changes had a special impact on theology.

"The first view was that the bible had grown up over many centuries, and that many strands and threads were woven into it, that it was not directly or verbally inspired by God, and that it had inconsistencies of data and dating, and that it showed a clear evidence of the growing understanding of the nature and the plan of God. The bible could, therefore, be studied and analysed by the methods applied to any work of history or literature".

The writer goes on to say that the second impact came from the amazing growth of scientific knowledge. More and more secrets of the universe were being unlocked and "what had seemed mysterious and unworkable became part of the corpus of knowledge . . . " Miracles just did not happen.

This was heady stuff in 1904. Hooper had been given absolute freedom in the pulpit and he used this. His controversial views caused strains among his congregation and one Sunday afternoon he preached a memorable sermon which he later had published. A copy can be seen in the Norris Museum. Hooper talked of "the present theological storm which is sweeping nonconformist thought". He deplored the fact that the issue had been clouded by personalities and defended Campbell. He swiped at "the sensational methods of the halfpenny Press in forcing this matter upon the public" and spoke of "detached and multilated" passages from Campbell's sermons being used to ridicule the new thinking.

During Hooper's ministry Campbell preached in St Ives from time to time and drew large audiences. Special trains were laid on from Godmanchester. Perhaps it was not Hooper's fault that church finances went through a lean time during his ministry. At one stage he offered to take a cut in salary but his offer was declined. Things improved and a manse was built in Tenterleas. Hooper left in June 1917, but died from blood poisoning six months later. His body was brought back to St Ives for burial.

All Saints' church can claim Hunt and Father Algy as two outstanding personalities. The Free Church can also notch up two in Potto Brown and the Rev. Wilfred Bonsey. This absent minded minister came to St Ives in 1927. His ministry was punctuated with a series of mishaps. It got off to a querulous start. The deacons had agreed to meet his moving costs, but these were so high, he was told he must pay half. His belongings included a large wooden garage in which he proposed not only to house his car but also the family's pet goat.

His wife was an artist, totally uninterested in church affairs. This in itself was bad enough, but she did not endear herself to the other wives by keeping hens and rabbits in the manse and leaving a light on all night for them. Bonsey was a bespectacled optimist and enthusiastic about his work. The deacons disagreed with some of the changes he wished to make, mainly on cost grounds, as finances were low owing to the approaching depression.

Though the new minister had his differences with the deacons, he was popular with the younger members of the congregation. Like Father Algy he encouraged them to take a full part in church affairs. At one church meeting a letter signed by 31 young members was read out protesting at the attitude of some of the deacons to Bonsey.

Bonsey did not help his cause by possessing a dreadful memory. His wife refused to organise his diary, and brides were left sobbing before the altar, stood up, not by their bridegrooms, but by an absent cleric. Bereaved relatives were apt to have their distress compounded when they arrived with the coffin to find no one present to conduct the funeral service. It was reported that he not only forgot to mark the children's scripture examination papers, but was not above losing them altogether. New strains developed. Some members complained that the choir was no good and some stayed away from services.

The year 1936 was a busy year for the church, and for some the best news was that Bonsey was resigning to join the Church of England. The deacons passed a resolution wishing him

"God speed and all happiness", but one gets the impression their hearts were not really in this charitable message. A major change took place in 1971 when the Congregationalists and the Presbyterians joined forces nationally to unite in a new body called the United Reformed Church, though the term Free Church is still freely used in St Ives. It was proposed that the Methodists should also join, but there were disagreements, and a decision was, and remains, deferred.

In 1976 plans for reconstructing the church were drawn up. The main idea was to ensure more efficiency and to extend the premises to allow the letting of part of the church for shops. The final cost of alterations was £178,000 of which about half was met by the Manpower Services Commission. An appeal was made for £40,000, and within a month half that amount had been contributed by church members and friends. The town council also gave £5,000 and Cambridge County Council £21,000.

While work was going on, the minister received a letter apparently from the manager of the Golden Lion, alleging that a workman had been leering at a woman guest from a window. The writer said the woman would be discussing the matter with the manager that afternoon and suggested that the minister attend. The minister and two church members prepared to go before one of them worked out that the signature was an anagram of April Fool. The work was completed in 1980 and on September 27th that year was re-opened under its new name, the Free Church Centre.

In the County Record Office in Huntingdon there is a large book of which less than a quarter has been used. It contains the names of members during the late nineteenth century. A final terse entry in 1904 states: "See new church book". Inside the flyleaf are two notes signed by the Rev. Thomas Lloyd, minister in 1867. The first reads: "Mr. Holland informed me that one, Braford, took away the church books which contained the records of the first planting of this church. These disappeared and it is presumed they were burnt after Braford died".

The second reads: "Mr. Holland thinks the 'cause' at St Ives, i.e. the church, originated from the preaching of Messrs Holcroft and Oddy whose remains lie in a garden at Longstanton." Both notes are dated 1867. Also inside the flyleaf is pasted a small piece of paper with a scribbled note in parts difficult to read. This note is also signed by Lloyd and says: "The Presbyterian chapel had its origin during the time of the Civil War in the reign of Charles when the ejected minister of St Ives, Henry Downett, who was the vicar, was supported by the inhabitants in opposition to the existing government. The Rev. Henry Downett was sequestrated in 1642 and was succeeded by Welsted (?) in 1650. This paper was put in my hands in 1866". It seems Lloyd mistook Downett for Downhale who was vicar at the time he is talking about.

The Rev. Leonard John Ballard, who was minister from 1949 to 1974, and at 79 still lives in St Ives, says Holcroft and Oddy are buried in Oakington and not at Longstanton. Oddy was related to Ruth Harrison who married Jack Harrison, the St Ives basket maker. He and Holcroft were constantly arrested and gaoled for preaching without a licence. Holcroft spent the period 1663 to 1672 in a Cambridge jail, but evidently had a kindly gaoler who let him out occasionally, as there are records of him preaching in 1669.

On the first page proper of the book it is recorded that Francis Goodison Panting, who had been pastor more than 40 years, and had succeeded David Jennings, resigned in 1811, and in turn was succeeded by Thomas Steffe Crisp. He died in April 1818 aged 77. There follows the first list of members. As the century progresses, names familiar in the town today begin to appear. They include Norris, Ulph, Warren, Bryant and Harrison.

Another vestry book contains a cutting from the *Eastern Counties Gazette* dated October 17th, 1863, giving a report of the dedication of the new chapel. The architect was John Tarring of London. The report describes the spire as early Gothic and says it was 156 feet high. When the foundation stone was laid, the paper adds, a glass vase was fitted into a cavity. In this were placed some daily newspapers, a short history of the old chapel and some coins.

This glass vial was taken out in August 1973 during renovation work and a new stainless steel cylinder inserted into the cavity. Into it were placed a copy of that day's *Times* and a full range of coins. The cylinder was filled with inert gas to prevent damage from damp. The old cylinder had been found intact, but water had seeped into it and the newspaper and the history had been irreparably damaged. The coins were retrieved. It is now in the possession of John Ballard.

Despite a recent serious illness, he still cycles and drives round the town. Born in Bishop's Stortford he went to Cheshunt College, Cambridge and was ordained in 1932. He is a widower. His first ministry was at Sawston and he came to St Ives from Harpenden. From St Ives he went to Hunstanton and has lived in a retirement home since 1980. He has a son, two daughters and four grandchildren.

His successor, still the minister, was the Rev. Donald McIllhaga, whose wife, Kate, is also the Free Church's community minister. Born in the Wirral, he is 56 and read philosophy at Dublin University. He spent two years in the army intelligence corps and went on to take his theological training at Westminster College. He was on the staff of the Student Christian Movement in Leeds and Sheffield for four years and then minister in Sheffield for a further seven. Later he moved to Bar Hill and was also on the staff of Swavesey Village College as a school counsellor before coming to St Ives in January 1975.

He has seen the town change dramatically, particularly citing the enormous growth in population over the last fifteen years. He recalls his first glimpse of the "Victorian pseudo Gothic" of his new church. The church was at that time dim with the windows fitted with dark green glass.

The new minister realised soon after his arrival that there was a large gulf between the anglicans and the nonconformists in the town. One morning he was approached on Market Hill by Bill Harrison, a leading light in the Civic Society and an anglican. He was a diminutive man and as he introduced himself to McIllhagga, he drew himself up to his full height and declared: "Just remember, we are the royalists".

The minister has always pressed for the church to take an active part in the community and was pleased when two shops were opened on the ground floor. The decision to reconstruct the interior of the church to allow for its multiple use was taken on November 5th, 1978 in front of a congregation which was the largest seen for a long time. There were 124 members and between 20 and 30 adherents present. The voting was 112 for with only 12 against. Membership is rising and congregations have also swelled in recent years. "We are the third strongest URC in Cambridgeshire, the other two being in Cambridge itself", the minister says.

Chapter 14
Other Churches

Methodists can trace their history in St Ives back for more than two centuries. The seeds of Methodism in the town were sown by John Wesley. That daunting preacher was touring the fens in November 1774 and was being driven in a horse chaise one stormy night from Sutton to Earith. The weather was so bad the driver "crept along over the fen banks", and finally had to get down and lead the horse through squelching, calf-deep mud.

Eventually the chaise could not cope. Wesley borrowed a horse from a farmhouse but after a while the road became impassable. Somehow the preacher procured a boat and a youth paddled him to his destination. There a "Miss L" drove him to St Ives. Wesley confided to his journal: "No Methodist, I was told, had preached in this town, so I thought it was high time to begin, and at about one I preached to a well dressed and yet well behaved congregation". This is a curious sentence. It appears to indicate that nonconformist preachers were often heckled and interrupted by wealthy people who tended to be Anglican. Dissenters at that time appealed mainly to the poor.

The seed Wesley planted flourished. For a while the St Ives converts became part of the Bedford circuit. In 1793 it became the head of a circuit and in 1800 was incorporated into the St Neots circuit. Twelve years later the St Ives and Huntingdon circuit, which at that time included Ramsey, was formed. In 1815, the year of Waterloo, a chapel was built in the town and was used for the next 89 years. Several famous preachers came to St Ives. The chapel originally had a small graveyard both in front of the building and at the back.

The chapel was pulled down in 1904 to allow for a new building on the same site with a Sunday School attached. The cost was £4,000 and the new school opened in September 1904. The chapel was dedicated the following year. The total cost was £5,300. In March 1888 there were 297 members in the circuit, an increase of 25 on the previous year. There were also 108 people on trial for membership.

The Huntingdonshire mission was formed at the 1903 national conference by unifying the circuits previously known as the St Ives and Huntingdon circuits, the St Neots circuit and the Ramsey circuit. By December 1903 the membership of this body was 858 with 26 triallists.

Wesley cared passionately for the societies he founded. The son of an Anglican clergyman from Lincolnshire, he went to Oxford and began life with high church views. Ian Suttie, whose parents live in St Ives, and who is a Methodist minister in Maldon, Essex, wrote a thesis on Wesleyan Methodism in the town between 1850 and 1910 when he was studying for a history degree at York University.

By and large the social status of the first Methodists was not high. The religion appealed to the poor. In 1792 they bought a barn and it was on this site that the St Ives Methodists were to build their first chapel. The relative poverty of the Methodists can be seen by comparing the lifestyle of their clergy with that of Anglican vicars. In the mid nineteenth century the Rev. Yate Fosbrooke, the Anglican vicar of St Ives, lived in a rambling parsonage with his wife, three children and four servants. His Wesleyan counterpart lived alone with no servants.

Furnishing their minister's house was the responsibility of members of the society and a document dated 1891 shows the St Ives minister led a hard life. The contents of his sitting room consisted of one linoleum floor cloth, a steel fender, a set of five chairs, a dining table, one table cloth, a pair of lace curtains, three shelves, a stool and a lamp. Six years later this meagre furniture had been supplemented and the minister indulged in the luxury of a couch. A further six years on the original furniture was still in the room, but the couch had gone.

Methodist ministers also received poor salaries. A national census in 1851 discloses that while the average Anglican vicar received £300 a year, a married Primitive Methodist minister could expect only 19 shillings a week. By the winter of 1894 conditions in the manse had become intolerable and the minister sent a heartfelt plea to his trustees. His main complaint was that "the water from the well at the house is thoroughly unfit (being impregnated with worms) for drinking purposes and I have not been able to use it for months". The trustees laid on a new supply of water and, while they were at it, agreed to replace a stove and make a few minor alterations.

By 1874 a small breakaway group calling themselves Primitive Methodists had been formed and was holding separate services conducted by what one anonymous and jaundiced observer described as "converted gypsies". Members of the new group were motivated by the fact they felt Methodists were becoming too close to the Establishment. By the end of the century the two groups were growing closer together and they finally united in 1932 and became the United Methodist Church. In the west country the Primitive Methodists had been known as Bible Christians.

Like Methodists throughout the country, those in St Ives tried to exert a good influence on society. They participated in organisations of which they approved and made vigorous efforts to get on the council. They exerted a major influence by becoming closely involved with the national Band of Hope movement, established by members of the Temperance Movement.

The United States claims to have been the birthplace of the Temperance Movement. A number of societies grew up there during the early part of the nineteenth century, campaigning against drinking spirits and wines. But this "moderation" system was not good enough for fervent teetotallers, and in 1826 the American minister the Rev. Calvin Chapin, published a series of articles on "total abstinence the only infallible antidote".

By 1829 the movement had spread to Britain and societies began to be established. Preston was the first town in England to have a society, and on September 1, 1832 seven leading figures in the town took the following pledge: "We agree to abstain from all liquors of an intoxicating quality, whether ale, porter, wine or ardent spirits, except as medicines".

Exactly when the Temperance cause was first propounded in St Ives is not known, but it appears to have been about 1843. The first three openly to declare their adherence were George Norris, T Phillips and J B Childs. Meetings were held from time to time in one of the schools. Efforts were made to influence children to forswear alcohol, and a Band of Hope group was established. This met in the vestry of the Wesleyan church.

Wesleyans at that time had mixed views about the Temperance Movement. Some favoured teetotalism, but others were not opposed to alcohol in moderation. Some indeed distrusted the fervour which teetotalers brought to their cause and the impassioned speeches they made. Others objected to the use of the vestry for Temperance meetings.

By 1848 the society had developed sufficiently for members to feel they could unite into a formal body and in April of that year the first annual meeting of the St Ives Temperance Society was held at which officers and members of committees were elected. It was agreed to hold an annual Good Friday Festival. The Society rented rooms in the Broadway where monthly meetings were held and one of their first decisions was to subscribe to the *Teetotal Times* and the *Temperance Recorder*. By the 1860s the Society was accepted as part of the town's life. Its festival was a major event and had become one of the town's institutions.

The Band of Hope attracted a wide range of children and meetings for them were organised by Thomas Phillips, a fruiterer and trustee of the society. The Methodists gradually grew closer to the Society. Phillips joined it in 1845 and came perilously close to being expelled by the Methodists for his fierce teetotal views. He declaimed against alcohol at

Fig. 18. Pugin's Church of the Sacred Heart, moved to St Ives in 1902 (*above*); and the Methodist Chapel of 1905.

public meetings and abstained from communion because of his abhorrence of "fermented wine". Methodists at that time were more tolerant. Some even felt total abstainers could suffer "annoyance from teetotalism", and were unimpressed by the "intemperate and exciting talk of teetotal advocates".

But by the time time Phillips attained a position of authority as the Band of Hope supervisor, things had changed dramatically. By then teetotalism was identified with nonconformity and particularly with Wesleyanism.

Children were warned of the perils of alcohol from an early age. They were urged to learn jingles which encouraged them to renounce alcohol. A copy of the Book of Reciter used at a festival in St Ives at the turn of the century illustrates this. One recitation reads:

> Come alcohol, now answer me,
> The question I shall put to thee.
> What is thy trade, what is thy name?
> My age it is four thousand years,
> My aim to fill the earth with tears,
> My trade to kill and make expense,
> My trade it is intemperance.

The recitation concludes with an appeal from the reciters:

> Then boys and girls be wide awake,
> Your foe begins to fear and quake,
> Stand to your post! Go hand in hand,
> And drive this monster from our land.

Apart from virtually running the Band of Hope, Methodists were active in other ways trying to influence St Ivians to cut down on the hard stuff, or better still, abandon alcohol completely. Alcoholism tended to be a serious problem. In the late nineteenth ceentury there were 72 public houses in the town whose boundaries were miniscule compared with those today. St Ives also had at least two breweries. The annual fair posed problems for the anti-drink lobby. To counter it the British Womens Temperance Association ran an alcohol free refreshment tent.

Temperance was an emotive issue and Wesleyans adopted a catchphrase declaring their intention of "outflanking the publican". They organised teas and entertainments, they sought recruits in public houses. Their members on the council exerted all the influence they could muster. The Movement stabilised in the early part of this century, but the outbreak of the First World War marked a decline in its strength from which it never recovered.

Methodists were very strongly in favour of a complete observance of the sabbath and they protested in the summer of 1917 when the government urged farmers to work their ploughmen on Sundays in the interests of the nation's food requirements. The Huntingdonshire mission sent a message to prime minister Lloyd George urging him to allow Sunday to be a day of rest.

The present minister, 31-year-old Mark Goodhand, believes Methodism is strong in St Ives today. He says the movement is "picking up again" after some years when it stagnated. The average Sunday congregation numbers about 95. A married man with two daughters, he went to Queen's Theological College in Birmingham. St Ives is his first ministry.

The minister maintains the Methodists have a foot in both camps – the Anglicans and the Free Church. He preaches that the gospel is for everyone and that everybody can be saved. He also thinks St Ives is a an ecumenical town and strongly upholds the view that there must be no alcohol and no gambling on Methodist premises.

The seventeenth century also witnessed the birth of the Quaker movement in St Ives.

Records are sketchy, but it is known that Quakers first established themselves in Huntingdonshire at Earith in 1657. Norris says that a year later there was a group of Friends in St Ives. The noted Quaker, George Fox visited the county frequently and in his journal gives an account of a visit in 1656. He writes: "The mayor of Huntingdon came to see me, and was very loving, and his wife received the truth". Fox came to the county again in 1659, 1662, 1668, 1669 and, for the last time, in 1678. He notes: "I went to Huntingdon in which county I staid several days, having many meetings. At St Ives George Whitehead came to see me, and travelled with me in the work of the Lord for five or six days in that county".

The Quakers suffered persecution for their refusal to attend the established church, and there are many records of punishment or "sufferings" as the Quakers described them. Some of these are in the County Record Office in Shire Hall, Cambridge. We read: "1670. Robert Ingram of St Ives and John Peacock of the same, were arrested by a byshop's writ, and had to the county gaol in Huntingdon where they continued about 18 months, and then were released by Act of Parliament".

For the same year another entry states: "The 15th day of the 3rd month a meeting held by Thomas Ibott was disturbed. Most of those present were fined. Tobias Hardmeat of Fenstanton paid 5s for himself and £5 for the house, because Thomas was poor. Samuel Nottingham paid 5s and £5, and Thomas Parnell also. The Conventicle Act required each person to pay 5s and the whole house £20. Reuben Eldred, who was present, could not pay the 5s fine and so a kettle was taken from him, value 8s. From John Parnell they took four bushels of malt; from John Apthorpe a warming pan and pewter dish 7s; Daniel Abott a new lantern, and so forth". Parnell and Abott also incurred fines at Godmanchester.

In 1683 on "The 29th day of the tenth month, Tobias Hardmeat committed to gaol for refusing tithes". The sufferings of the Friends were severe. In 1780 fines amounting to £222.4.4d were levied in St Ives alone.

There are several accounts of a bizarre incident involving the recalcitrant Ibott. He went to live in London in 1666. There, two days before the great fire, he wandered about the city in dishevelled clothes "as though he had just risen from bed, pronouncing a judgement by fire which should lay waste the city". Possibly unable to suppress a glow of pride when his prediction was fulfilled within forty-eight hours, he rushed out of doors with arms outstretched as though attempting to arrest the flames. Wiser counsels prevailed and "he was moved from destruction by his friends".

There are scarcely any local records of the history of the Roman Catholic Church in St Ives. The present church in Needingworth Road, was dismantled and transported to St Ives in 1902. Professor Philip Wilkins of Cambridge writes:

"After the Reformation period, Sawston Hall, where the resident Huddleston family maintained allegiance to the old faith over succeeding centuries, provided the only continuous centre in Cambridgeshire for Catholics to practise their religion. It was from here that the main effort to launch a Catholic Mission in Cambridge came in the 1830s after Catholic Emancipation. Major Richard Huddleston acquired land in Union Road in the Newtown area, and the Church of St Andrew, built to a design of Augustus Welby Pugin, was consecrated on St George's Day 1843. It occupied a site on which buildings of St Alban's Roman Catholic School now exist.

"The church was notable as being Pugin's first design after his conversion to Catholicism in 1835. A lithograph of the time shows how, in the interior, an attempt was made to create a sense of spaciousness beyond the obvious restriction of a small building by use of a steeply-pitched central roof and short arcades to small aisles of equal length to the nave. The sanctuary was separated from the nave by an open screen surmounted by a rood.

"After it was replaced in 1890 by the larger church of Our Lady and the English Martyrs, St Andrew's became redundant and in 1902 was dismantled and transported by barge to St Ives. There in 1900 Mr George Pauling of London, a native of St Ives and a convert to

Catholicism, had bought a plot of land with a wooden hall upon it in East Street. The hall was used as a chapel, later known as "the Studio". Mr Pauling bought another plot of land in Needingworth Road and paid for removing and re-erecting the old Church of St Andrew from Cambridge on that site. The architects involved were Mr Morley of Cambridge and Mr Robb of St Ives and the builders were Messrs F. B. Thackeray of Huntingdon.

"When re-erected at St Ives, a clerestory was added to the church and in recent years a dual-purpose area has been built on to the north side. Judging from a description of the church written in 1851, the altar is the original one built of Caen stone, a central quatrefoil bearing the figure of the Lamb with symbols of the four Evangelists and quatrefoils on either side with figures of winged angels".

The church is now called the Sacred Heart of Jesus Christ, and its parish priest is Father Raymond Kerby. He came to St Ives in September 1981 from Hadleigh, near Ipswich. Born in Ipswich, Father Kerby took his theological degrees in Rome and was ordained in St John Lateran, the cathedral of the Italian capital.

In the summer he holds masses every Monday morning in the chapel on the bridge and draws congregations of about 30. They consist mainly of retired people, but Monday morning shoppers also come. "I hold the masses there because that was the reason for which it was built", Father Kerby observes. "It is being put to the use for which it was built. It has a special attraction. Even the ducks join in".

His church can hold about 240, and he has more than 200 every Sunday morning and again in the evening. He believes Roman Catholicism has grown stronger in the area in recent years because of the influx of people, particularly those from the north and Scotland.

Chapter 15
A Century of Borough Status

For exactly a hundred years St Ives was a borough. It was granted this status in 1874, and lost it under a Local Government Act passed by prime minister Edward Heath's government in 1972, which came into effect two years later. The first mayor of the new town council, Fred Jennings, was elected on May 14, 1974.

The first meeting of the new borough council was held on November 9, 1874. Twelve councillors sat around the table: Read Adams, Harvey Goodman, John Edward, John Wadsworth, Thomas King, Cornelius Robinson, Robert Barton, William Wigston Warner, William Phillips, Thomas Child Tyson, Thomas Matthews and Henry Fromant.

Four men – Gilbert Ansley, George William Brown, Thomas Coote and Richard Wise – were elected aldermen, and George Newton Day was appointed town clerk. A latinist came up with the motto *sudore non sopore* – by labour and not sleep. Within two months the council got an unpleasant reminder of mortality when alderman Ansley died. He was replaced by Martin Osborne.

Members of the new body got busily down to work. They considered conditions under which shopkeepers would be permitted to store lighting fuel. There were to be not more than four gallons in any shop, and no more than 50 gallons in any building in which petrol was being stored. The council appointed an Inspector of Nuisances and Common Lodging Houses and a superintendent of fire engines, and decreed that these vehicles must carry lanterns at night.

By 1875 negotiations were opened with the Duke of Manchester to buy the market tolls, but councillors declined the first ducal price suggested as it was considered "more than 40 years purchase at the same time". It was decided to seek expert advice on how many years were normally paid for in the transfer of tolls. The council was told it was normally 18 to 20 years.

In 1878 the council was informed that the finances of both the elementary schools, the National and the British, were unsatisfactory and that they were likely to worsen. If they closed, a School Board would have to be set up. Under the Elementary Education Act of 1876 it was necessary to appoint an official to enforce attendance at school, and his duties had to be supervised either by an Attendance Committee or the School Board. The School Board would give ratepayers and parents some practical control over the schools.

Elementary schools were empowered to charge a minimum 3d a week for every child, a sum too high for some parents. If there were a School Attendance Committee, those parents would have to go before a Board of Guardians for help. Councillors felt this would be a "most objectionable course, tending to pauperise those who were compelled to make an application for aid". A School Board would have the power to remit part of the fee if members felt this was justified. It is plain the council was divided on this issue, because when it came to a vote it was decided by six votes to five with three abstentions to opt for an Attendance Committee.

The minutes are full of trivia, such as the regular use by boys of catapults to damage the Free Church clock, but there was also pleasant news. In October 1901 the council's attention was drawn to the fact that St Ives was becoming known as an angling resort. A long article had recently appeared in the national *Anglers News* praising the excellent fishing to be had on the banks of the Ouse. The author of the article had one reservation. The river at St Ives, he said, was weedy and very dirty. He urged the authorities to remedy this. He wrote: "The river at St

Ives runs through a picturesque country and holds, so far as angling is concerned, a splendid stock of fish. St Ives ought to be a great fishing and boating centre, a much frequented resort for holiday makers. No district affords more facilities in this direction".

He went on to detail all the fish that could be found, such as roach, pike, dace, perch, bream, chubb, rudd, tench, trout, carp and barbel. He predicted that if only angling conditions were improved, St Ives could become another Staines or Datchet. The council discussed this matter at a number of meetings, but there is no record to suggest that a concerted effort to attract more anglers was ever made.

The following year a letter was sent to the Home Secretary asking for new laws which would allow the council to carry out work to avoid serious flooding, and the council also gratefully accepted the gift of a drinking fountain which stands in the Broadway. It was given to the town by Elliot Odams to commemorate Queen Victoria's diamond jubilee. Though this tribute was five years late an installation ceremony was held and the donor was effusively thanked.

As war in Europe threatened, the borough council met regularly to discuss what action they should take to help the war effort should the worst come to the worst.

The council, one of whose members rejoiced in the name of George Gabriel Glasspool Wheeler, went on conducting its business quietly. They were keeping an eye on the town's health and deep into sanitation matters when St Ives was rocked by a dramatic murder and suicide in the Temperance Hotel in Crown Street.

On a bleak Saturday night in February 1913, a servant girl found the body of her mistress, Elizabeth Warnes, manageress of the hotel then owned by the Kiddle family, lying dead on the floor of her living room in her flat above the hotel. Sprawled across her was the body of a German friend of hers, Gustav Kunne.

Each had died as the result of a single stab wound. Kunne used to come to England from his home in Germany each year during the chicory season to work in a Fenstanton factory. The discovery of the bodies caused a sensation in the town where Mrs Warnes was well known. Before she had separated from her husband, the couple had run the Cow and Hare public house. After the split Warnes left the district and his wife took over the running of the Temperance Hotel.

She had become friendly with Kunne, who was a frequent visitor to her flat and though she ran the hotel, she did not extend into her private life the principles for which the establishment stood. She and Kunne were regularly to be seen in the town's hotels and public houses. On the night of the tragedy they had been seen in a public house near the railway. The inquest was a lengthy one which drew large crowds with the jury bringing in the inevitable verdict that Kunne had killed his companion before turning the knife on himself. The inquest was held two days after the bodies had been discovered, and the corpses were left lying as they had been found so that members of the jury could see the scene for themselves.

In 1917 another tragedy, this time involving the Copley family shocked the town. Copley and Sons is still one of St Ives' most respected firms of solicitors though the Copley family is no longer directly involved. In March 1917 seven-year-old George Copley drowned in a well while his parents, who lived at Green End, were attending the funeral of his grandfather, Robert Mackley Copley, manager of Barclays Bank.

The boy had been considered too young to attend the funeral and had been taken for a walk by his governess in The Thicket where he discovered a disused well. He had wandered away from his governess who had stopped to talk to a young soldier she knew and must have prised open the lid, lost his balance and fallen in.

In the confusion that followed the discovery of his disappearance, it was some hours before Charles Hobbs, the gardener at Houghton Grange and one of the few people who knew where the well was, could be found and the body retrieved. Until his arrival the boy's father, Harry Copley, and police officers searched frantically to find it, while the governess sobbed in the house. Three days after his grandfather's funeral, George Copley was buried alongside him.

George's brother, Bob Copley, now 87, can still vividly recall the tragedy. He maintains the governess was engaged in an association involving more than conversation at the time of the accident. "When we returned from the funeral all hell broke loose", he recalls. "My mother collapsed and my father joined police who were already combing The Thicket. I shall never forget the moment when George's body was recovered. The governess was instantly sacked". Bob Copley is probably the only person in St Ives who knows where the well is. It is completely covered and securely fastened and lies just beyond the eighth green on the town's golf course.

In August 1919 the first signs appeared that the town was expanding. The council agreed to build 42 houses on a site between Ramsey Road and Houghton Road. Twenty four would face Ramsey Road and would be for workmen. The rest would look out to Houghton Road and would be for "artisans".

That same year on a bitterly cold December evening, a thinly attended public meeting was held to discuss suggestions for a war memorial to commemorate St Ivians killed in battle. A committee had already recommended the erection of a memorial on Market Hill and the laying out of an embankment garden along The Waits. During the war 467 young men had joined up and 60 of them had died. The town's population at the time was about 3,000.

Mayor John Johnson said that for some years the town had been raising money at the rate of more than £1,000 a year for war charities and if the same amount could be raised during the next twelve months, the cost of a memorial could be met. He suggested the memorial should be called the Cross of Sacrifice and that it should have the names of those who died inscribed on it.

Some nonconformists at the meeting were unhappy at the idea of having the memorial in the shape of a cross, and an obelisk was suggested as an alternative. One man, Ernest Culpin, ruminated on what Oliver Cromwell would think of having to look out at a cross forever, and the meeting became a little heated. Several amendments were voted upon and defeated, and the original plan received a large majority. After the meeting the acerbic Mr Culpin was left muttering that the whole thing had been cut and dried before the meeting started and it did not matter what other people thought.

The year 1919 also witnessed a move to get the Michaelmas Fair moved from the centre of the town, a move that was to be repeated for many years. This fair, already old in Edmund Pettis' time, was not instituted by a charter, and so the precise date on which it was first held is unknown. Some of the town's traders felt that the fair disrupted normal business, but their plea to move it elsewhere was rejected.

The medical officer's report for 1919 disclosed that the past 12 months had been particularly wet with a heavier than average rainfall. It also showed the town's population was 2,991 and mentioned a surprising fact. There had been two cases of malaria. One patient had been to Africa where he would have been exposed to the disease, but the other patient had never been abroad in his life. The report stated: "This case was investigated by a government inspector who found the particular mosquito which carries the disease breeding extensively in the river a few yards from the patient's door". The council was assured the matter had been efficiently dealt with and the mosquitoes exterminated.

In 1921 the council agreed to place a German gun, given to it after the war, on the green along The Waits facing towards the meadow. It was sold to an unknown buyer in 1932. At the same time members noted a nationwide appeal to economise on coal, coke and gas because of a shortage. A Coal Emergency committee was formed and the council agreed that only those public lamps absolutely necessary for safety were to be lit.

In the spring of 1921 the council finally acquired the bridge tolls from the Duke of Manchester and immediately stopped imposing them, thereby putting an end to an anomaly which had caused illwill for several years. When the abbot of Ramsey Abbey built the first wooden bridge, he presumably imposed tolls, though there is no record of this. When the stone bridge was constructed, tolls were certainly levied, the bridge chapel having been built not solely for religious purposes, but also for the collection of money.

With the Dissolution of the Monasteries in 1539 the bridge became a Crown possession, and was passed to various members of the royal family. The Dukes of Manchester acquired the bridge along with a good deal more of the town in the seventeenth century, and successive dukes continued to levy the tolls. During the last century this led to some resentment, and it is clear that by the 1890s St Ives residents were exempt from paying tolls, but that it was still levied on visitors.

This created confusion and also heightened the resentment felt by farmers in the surrounding area. Some St Ives traders were worried that the tolls were driving business elsewhere. The opening of a new, modern market in Cambridge in 1886 increased their apprehension. Excitable meetings were held on Market Hill at which people demanded that the council should purchase the tolls and stop levying them.

Council members in general agreed with this view, but vacillated and had not acquired the tolls when war broke out in 1914. What happened during the next few years is unclear, but it is a fact that by the time the war ended the tolls, while still officially in effect, were not being collected.

It was in this situation that the council, having erected a war memorial and laid out a lawn in memory of the town's dead, once more turned its attention to the problem, and a meeting held in April 1921 finally dealt with it. At the end of the war some of the duke's estates, including the tolls, came up for auction, and the council authorised mayor George Wheeler and two other members to negotiate on its behalf.

A lengthy set of talks then developed with the duke's agent after the tolls were withdrawn from the auction. It was pointed out that the responsibilities involved in maintaining the bridge were substantial, and it was agreed these would have to be taken over by the county council. Another set of talks then started with this body. After months of discussion the matter was finally resolved. The borough council acquired the tolls and stopped imposing them.

In May 1921, Dr Reggie Grove reported that the town's population was 3,015. He also assured council members that the water supplied by the East Hunts Co. was good and that only a few houses still relied on well water. Nearly all the privies had gone. About a third of the residents still relied on the pail system for sanitation and the night cart was still required. More water closets were being installed. There had been 56 cases of diphtheria following an epidemic which had started in Huntingdon. St Ives had five registered slaughter houses.

Street lighting caused the council concern during the 1920s, and in November 1921 they were shocked when their newly-elected mayor, Joseph Ingram, died suddenly after only one month in office. John Johnson, who had just retired as mayor, was elected for a second term. Early in 1921 the council decided not to pay £80 for a steam fire engine as councillors felt the borough "is amply protected by the hydrant and the present manual."

At a special council meeting in January 1924 a suggestion was put forward that was to split the council and lead to angry public meetings. The mayor, Christopher Ingram, said he had received an offer from Lloyds Bank to sell their premises at Stanley House to the council for £1,200. The house, on Market Hill, had been owned for years by the Warner family who had sold it to Lloyds Bank who at that time were looking for temporary accommodation while their present premises were being built.

The mayor remarked: "The premises would make an admirable municipal building with very little if any structural alteration being necessary". He added that the only real alteration required was the provision of toilet facilities for both men and women. After estimates had been received it became known that the total cost of buying and altering the house would be £1,440, with an additional £320 for toilet facilities.

The issue provoked widespread argument in the town, and the council's medical officer, Dr Reggie Grove, headed a deputation on behalf of residents to oppose the move. He handed in a petition signed by 300 ratepayers deploring the buying of Stanley House. This was presented to the council at a meeting which also had before it letters from two ailing councillors expressing strong disapproval. After a long discussion, the town clerk, George Dennis Day, was instructed to apply for government permission to go ahead with the purchase.

Another group of ratepayers saw the mayor, this time armed with a petition signed by 860 residents. It was agreed to invite five ratepayers to meet the council, but this invitation was declined on the grounds that it would not be helpful. The ratepayers said they would send a delegation to London to see the responsible minister.

By now an organisation calling itself the Ratepayers Association had been formed headed by several prominent St Ivians. They argued that buying Stanley House would result in a rate increase. A public enquiry was ordered and the debate when this was held, was fierce with both sides employing counsel. The association organised yet another petition, this time bearing 1,000 signatures, about a third of the population.

In June 1924 the government approved the purchase and also said the council could borrow the necessary money, and a resolution to go ahead was tabled. The voting was eight in favour, four against with one abstention. The council then moved swiftly. They decorated the caretaker's flat, had toilet facilities built, and ordered a three-section council table and a flagstaff. On November 10th 1924 the council held its first meeting in its new home and agreed the building would be called The Council Building. It is now the Town Hall.

The matter was not over. Later that same month elections were held and the Ratepayers Association put up candidates against three councillors seeking re-election – George Wheeler, Herbert Oldman and Harry Stiles.

An angry group of councillors defended themselves in a statement. "The committee of the Ratepayers Association", the statement said, "was invited to meet the council and discuss the question, but refused to do so. They accepted the challenge of a government enquiry, but having done so, refused to accept the umpire's decision.

"It was proved that the price was below official valuation, the premises suitable, the position good and the opportunity exceptional". It added that the average ratepayer would only be asked to pay about one penny a month, and that only until the loan had been repaid. The election meetings that November were hectic, and when it came to the vote the three sitting councillors were defeated.

The confusion had still not died down when a month later a letter was received from the county council on a far less emotive subject. The letter stated that the Office of Works acting on a recommendation from the Ancient Monuments Board, had scheduled St Ives bridge as "a monument the preservation of which is of national importance". Four years later Frederic Warren and town clerk George Dennis Day provided the money to buy the chapel on the bridge and they gave it to the Huntingdonshire County Council which already owned the bridge itself.

Early in 1934 the council minuted its thanks to Mrs Olive Sutton who had recently given Ingle Holt Island to the town. The island had belonged to the family of George Wright-Ingle who was Lord of the manors of Hilton and Fenstanton and had been High Sheriff in 1905. He retired to Eastbourne where he died, when the island passed to his son. On his death it went to Mrs Sutton, Wright-Ingle's daughter. The island had been used earlier this century as an osier bed by local basket makers until cheap imports from Belgium put an end to this trade. In accepting the gift the council decided to name the island Ingle Holt.

The first signs of a possible war in Europe were noticed during the summer of 1936 and the borough council was heavily involved with the St Ives Rural District Council discussing air raid precaution schemes. After the Munich crisis two years later the council expressed its thanks for the way in which various organisations in the town had rallied to help.

Among appointments made was that of Freddy Favell as chief billeting officer. Freddy had left school at 14 and gone to work for solicitor George Dennis Day. In 1927 he was asked to work as assistant to Day in his capacities as town clerk and clerk to the magistrates. After war broke out he was appointed assistant town clerk and became a full time council employee. In 1927 he had a foot amputated but despite this handicap would daily mount the long flight of stairs at the Town Hall carrying enormous minute books. He worked for the council until 1960 when he returned to work for Day and Sons. He retired in 1968 and took a part time job with the council, finally retiring in 1974. He now lives with his daughter and son in law, Valerie and John Seymour.

During the war the council abandoned its monthly meetings. It was now meeting frequently. It organised the requisitioning of railings, and in the summer of 1941, it was advised that in the event of a heavy air raid on Cambridge, arrangements had been made for 1,000 people from that city to be taken in by St Ives for up to 48 hours. As the tide of war turned the council busied itself with such matters as post-war housing, the Troops Coming Home Fund and the return of evacuees to their homes.

At the first municipal election after the war, in November 1945, the first woman councillor, Minnie Hudson was elected. She was a local teacher. By her election victory she secured her niche in local history, but when she took her seat for the first time, oddly enough no mention was made of this fact or if mention was made, it was not minuted.

Victory celebrations were organised for June 1946. There was a dinner for all ex-servicemen and women on June 7th and the next day a united Thanksgiving service in the morning. There followed a large procession with decorated floats, a children's fancy dress parade with tea on Market Hill for the children and the elderly. Sports were organised in the afternoon. There was an historical pageant, dancing in a floodlit Broadway and a torchlight procession. The festivities concluded with fireworks and a bonfire on Ingle Holt.

In December 1948 the council arranged to borrow £7,800 to buy the Corn Exchange and five years later decided to have a mace made. It was felt only about £150 could be spent and the London Goldsmiths and Silversmiths Co said a reasonable one could be made for that amount. Town clerk George Lewis Day said a much better one could be bought for about £250. He asked the council to deduct this amount from his salary for the next year to pay for the civic symbol. He said that if the mace cost more he would make up the difference. In the end the cost was £300.

The Day family had an unbroken record of service to the council stretching back almost a century. George Newton Day had been the borough's first clerk until 1890 when his son, George Dennis took over and served for the next fifty years. In 1940 his son, George Lewis succeeded his father and served until his retirement in 1960.

The year 1959 witnessed another serious attempt to get the Michaelmas Fair moved. A petition signed by residents and traders in Broadway, Merrylands and Crown Street talked of: "1. Serious inconvenience to all concerned. 2. Fire risk. 3. The possibility of damage to property and 4. Excessive traffic congestion in East Street and North Road". This issue dragged on until 1961 when a plebiscite was held. The voting showed that 462 residents were in favour of leaving the fair in the town centre while 223 wanted it moved.

In May 1962 Mary Grove was elected the first and, as it transpired the only woman alderman of the borough. She had been on the council for several years and had been mayor. Her family had a distinguished record of council service. Her grandfather Dr William Grove and her father Reggie had been successive medical officers for half a century.

The family came from the west country and moved to St Ives in the 1860s. Mary Grove grew up at Slepe House on Cromwell Terrace. It was said that whenever her father had

Fig. 19. Three Freemen of St Ives: (*above*) George Lewis Day and Bert Burgess; (*below left*) Douglas Bryant. Also Freddy Favell (*below right*), for many years assistant town clerk.

another child he built an extra room. If this was so, his building programme must have been extensive for he had seven daughters and three sons. Mary Grove still lives in the town. For several years she ran Tenterleas School and then went to India where she taught in Kashmir. She resigned from the council in 1970 "because I feel *anno domini* is catching up with me". She is remembered for her incisive interventions in council debate. "If she had an opinion, she knew how to express it", a former colleague recalls. "She never said anything unless she had some pertinent point to make".

In 1968 the council also elected another woman mayor, Ethel Cuttill. She had been married to Ernest Holmes and she had been mayoress when he was mayor on four occasions. He died in 1958 and councillor Maurice Warren came to see his widow and asked her to stand for the council so that her husband's record of public service could be continued. She was elected in 1960 and when she was installed as mayor, Warren came up to congratulate her and remarked: "I have only one regret. That is that you have remarried and that your name is no longer Holmes". Ethel Cuttill started the Darby and Joan Club in 1947. It had seven members. Today it has 180. She sighs for the days when St Ives was a borough. "We could deal with so many things", she says. "Now everything is so remote. You don't know with whom you are dealing".

In December 1968 it was decided to build a new swimming pool at a cost of £100,760. Of this the council was to pay £38,325 with the county council and the rural district council paying the rest. A later estimate amended the cost to £95,330. There was a fierce debate about the site. Some councillors favoured a pool on Ingle Holt where an existing pool was sited. Eventually it was decided this site was not suitable. The new pool was opened in September 1970, near the golf course.

Bert Burgess was elected the last mayor of the borough for 1973/74. In one of its final acts the council conferred the freedom of the borough on the mayor and on Dougles Bryant. Town clerk George Lewis Day had been made the first freeman in 1965. Douglas Bryant had first joined the council in 1935 and Bert Burgess had also given many years of service to the town.

The inaugural meeting of the new town council was held in August 1973 and a second meeting the following month studied the powers and duties of the new body. Fred Jennings was elected the first mayor in May 1974. The following year brought a mayoral sensation when Peter Fraser, the mayor elect, woke up one morning just days before he was due to be installed, to discover that a Sunday newspaper was alleging he was associating with a witchcraft cult in Cambridge. The paper stated that the cult, the Mendean Institute, could be described as satanic. Fraser agreed he had attended some meetings of the institute, but declared he was ignorant of any Satanic connection. He resigned both from his position as mayor elect and from the institute, but was again elected to be mayor a few years later.

The first elections since the new council was formed were held in May 1976. A number of former borough councillors including Ethel Cuttill and Michael Barton did not stand for the new body. Several new people were elected for the first time. They included the present mayor Mark Plews and his deputy, Jean Chandler. Other newcomers still on the council were David Hodge and Peter Ratcliffe.

In 1977 the council bought the town hall from Huntingdonshire District Council for £40,000 with half the money to be paid when the transaction was completed and the other half on April 1, 1978.

Among those who did join the new council were Rex Wadsworth, Peter Anderson and Bertie (Taffy) James. The last two had been mayors of the borough.

Taffy James' year of office from 1970/71 had been marked by two major events. While he was mayor the railway line to St Ives was axed by Lord Beeching. Taffy James and a few colleagues carried an empty coffin down to the station and members of the council rode on the last train to leave St Ives. It went to March.

In February of 1971 Joe Bugner, then based in St Ives, took the British heavyweight title

Fig. 20. St Ives Town Council in 1989. *Standing, left to right:* Cllrs H. R. Wadsworth, D. A. Sillett, K. Reynolds, J. C. Vickery, Mrs. P. Newbon and D. F. Hodge; Mr. W. A. Newbound, Macebearer; Cllrs A. L. Whitlock, G. A. Shipp, Mrs. S. M. Green, M. A. Malik, Mrs. P. E. Pegram and P. G. Ratcliffe. *Seated, left to right:* Cllr B. P. James; Mr. A. P. Watson, Town Clerk; Cllr M. Plews, Town Mayor; Rev. J. D. Moore, Town Mayor's Chaplain; Cllr Mrs. J. Chandler, Deputy Town Mayor; Cllr P. T. Anderson.

when he won a controversial points decision over the exceptionally popular holder, Henry Cooper. The town gave the new champion a hero's welcome when he returned from London and he was given a civic banquet at Slepe Hall. Taffy James also opened the new fire station.

Taffy James forsook his native Wales when during the war he met his present wife, Dorothy, when he was stationed in the area. She came from Somersham and they married after the war. Taffy joined the chicory company as a fieldsman and remained with them until 1974 when the factory was closed down.

He recalls that chicory was widely grown in the fens and was an important crop. It was used for mixing with coffee. But by the 1970s the crop was becoming unprofitable.

The possibility that St Ives might be twinned with a German town was first mentioned in February 1976, the day when Bert Burgess died suddenly. Mayor Rex Wadsworth said a letter had been received from Cambridgeshire County Council which spoke of a group of "folk dancers, musicians, gymnasts, ballroom dancers and trick cyclists" from Landkreis Marburg Biedenkopf visiting England. The group were keen to present an evening's entertainment in the town. The idea was to create an interest in twinning. It was agreed that the group be invited to perform in St Ives.

During the 1970s the town grew dramatically. More and more houses were built on the Ramsey Road estate as more and more people were drawn to the town because of its easy access to London, Cambridge and Peterborough. The decade witnessed an explosion in the population which now stands at about 16,000.

The St Ivo Centre was opened in September 1974 and the town's bypass in October 1980. In May 1982 Sue Mead, now Sue Green, became the first woman mayor of the town council. The new post office in Bridge Street was opened in 1985.

The idea for a bypass for the town, first mooted in the late 1960s, sparked a controversy which involved all the local councils and the Civic Society, a body formed in 1968. Its secretary, Bill Harrison, played a leading role in opposing an official plan to build the bypass over Hemingford Meadow and ultimately joining up with Ramsey Road. The debate dragged on for years with the borough and county councils favouring what became known as the western route, and the Civic Society proposing an eastern way instead. Members of the society maintained that the western route would destroy the beauty of the meadow. In the end the eastern route was chosen. When the bypass was officially named in July 1989, it was named Harrison Way.

The town council today has 16 members, four of them women. The councillors represent a wide range of interests. The mayor, Mark Plews, is the computer manager of a Huntingdon company. The husband of his deputy, Jean Chandler, is a builder. The council boasts one geographical curiosity. Pru Pegram is a St Helenan, born and bred on the island to which Napoleon was exiled after Waterloo.

Her father was the harbour master there, and she came to England in 1945. Two years later she met and married Reg Pegram. They came to St Ives in 1972, and a year later they launched, together with their daughter Cathy the first free newspaper in the area, the *Town Crier*. It circulated in Huntingdon and St Neots as well as in St Ives. The Pegrams sold it in March 1985. The other two women on the council are Sue Green and Pree Newbon.

In two ceremonies held in 1988 and 1989, St Ives became twinned with the West German town of Stadtallendorf, which is about 60 miles north of Frankfurt. The first signing ceremony was held at a special meeting of the town council held in the St Ivo school on November 19, 1988. It was attended by the bürgermeister of Stadtallendorf, then Manfred Vollmer, and twenty five other representatives of the German town, together with about 250 people from St Ives representing various organisations in the town.

St Ives mayor Mark Plews outlined the background to the twinning, saying that the first contacts were made in 1951 when Jean Chandler visited the Landkreis as a school girl.

Contacts were continued, and in 1968 the St Ivo School began exchanges with its counterpart in the German town. From then on a number of organisations began to develop contacts.

The council had first discussed the matter in 1977, but did not go ahead with twinning at that time. Huntingdonshire District Council then twinned with the Landkreis Marburg Biedenkopf of which Stadtallendorf formed part. After an exchange of visits in 1988 between the two council towns, it was decided to go ahead with the twinning.

The mayor then took the twinning oath on behalf of the Town, and announced that the Bürgermeister would take an identical oath at a ceremony in Stadtallendorf the following April. Several members of the council travelled to Stadtallendorf for the ceremony together with representatives of various organisations in the town. During a three day visit to their twin town, members of the delegation stayed with West German families, toured the area and visited the town's Ferrero chocolate factory. Mayor Plews and Bürgermeister Vollmer planted an oak sapling in the town's park to symbolise the friendship between the two towns.

Chapter 16
1110 And All That

As I was going to St Ives . . . no one writing about the town can avoid at some point setting out at least the opening line of the jingle conjured up by an unknown man which has achieved immortality.

It is sometimes claimed, that piece of doggerel verse refers to St Ives in Cornwall, the popular resort which attracts painters and writers who tend to get themselves photographed in striking poses and thereby impart glamour to the Cornish village. There can be no doubt, however, that the man who had the bizarre encounter in a country lane with someone with seven wives each humping her feline luggage, was on his way to the great St Ives fair.

The BBC has recognised this. In its edition of *Down Your Way* broadcast on February 10, 1980, the jingle was recited by Mary Grove. She had recorded it, under the direction of Brian Johnson, in the chapel on the bridge. She was the first speaker in the programme.

St Ives also inspired Rupert Brooke to verse. In his poem on Grantchester, in which he heaps praise on his beloved village but writes unflattering things about other places in the area including Cambridge, he turns his attention to St Ives. Having gazed across the fields towards the market town he delivers his verdict:

Strong men have blanched and shot their wives,
Rather than send them to St Ives.

Perhaps the poet would amend his judgement were he to visit the town today. With its roots in Saxon history, it has witnessed startling events. It achieved fame in medieval times, it has survived floods and hurricanes, it has boasted a distinguished cattle market, and in the last two decades it has grown enormously. When the Second World War ended, its population hovered around 3,000. In the sixties that figure was almost doubled, and in the last 20 years it has risen to nearly 16,000. Development plans allow for the town to have a population of 20,000 by the end of the century.

Many things have changed. The fair expired as an international event centuries ago. Sheep, cattle and pigs are no longer bought and sold every Monday. Politically it is now a sedate town. Gone is the passion, invective and danger of the nineteenth century. Electors are no longer routinely maimed or killed during election time. Foreign secretary John Major sits on a Conservative majority of 27,044. It is the biggest Conservative majority in England and Scotland, and is surpassed only by three Labour majorities for Welsh seats. Mr. Major was first elected to the constituency in 1979, succeeding Sir David, now Lord Renton, who had held it for the Tories since the war.

If St Ivo does, from time to time, hover over his town to see how things are going, he cannot be displeased with what he sees. He must rejoice to see how prosperous St Ives has become and what a busy, bustling place it still becomes each Monday. Over the past 100 years the saintly eyes will have noticed one change with approval. The number of public houses has shrunk dramatically.

It is difficult to establish just how many there were at the turn of the century. Several people have maps listing them and the numbers vary. It is safe though to assume that a century ago the then tiny town had at least 72 public houses or ale bars. Today the entire town, which has spread far beyond its nineteenth century boundaries, has a mere baker's dozen.

There is one fact that might give the bearded patriarch pause. Had the town ended up being called Slepe St Ives, the old man would no doubt have approved entirely. He must certainly have had an affection for the scruffy little village that took him in and from which he conducted his ministry. The linking of Slepe with the name of the man who hauled the village out of obscurity, would have been an ideal union. Perhaps one day Slepe St Ives will be what the town is called.